"Chuck Hyde is one of [the finest leaders I] know. He has devoted [his career to leadership] and has a wonderful, [unique way of] communicating his ideas. Any leader could benefit greatly from reading this commonsense book—one that doesn't prescribe a "one-size-fits-all" approach like so many others before it have done."

—Mark C. Zweig
Entrepreneur in-Residence, SAM M. WALTON COLLEGE OF BUSINESS,
University of Arkansas

I'm blessed to count Chuck as a loyal friend and trusted counsel in all aspects of leadership. This book is not a repackage of leadership with new buzz words. It is a master class in applying honed principles to real-world scenarios in context that you will derive great value from digesting.

—Aaron J. Marshall,
Team Marshall Angus

Chuck is an Executive leader with a unique coaching perspective on a leader's development. Seasons of a leader's life will create a new coaching vocabulary. It influenced my mindset as a coach in reading the drafts! He has lived the role at the top and is humble and vulnerable in passing along his lessons and learnings. I have had the pleasure of watching his transition from Corporate Suite to another C Suite...... Coach.

—Judy Campbell
President, JC Strategies

Chuck Hyde is equal parts business consultant, observer, deep-thinker, and storyteller. His call to action around the different kinds of leadership needed for the different kinds of business seasons is a brilliant read. This book confirms his moniker of being "constructively provocative."

—Stacey Mason
Founder, The Improv Lab

Full of nuanced insights from someone who understands the complicated reality of running a business, *Seasons in Leadership: A Model for Adaptive Focus, Message, and Belief* offers a way of thinking that will benefit any CEO. The book combines a wide range of useful anecdotes and practical frameworks that can be applied to the full range of challenges leaders face."

—Charles R. Scott
Executive Mentor

Chuck Hyde has broad and deep leadership experience. It's in his blood from family to work. *Seasons in Leadership* provides a practical, plug-and-play toolset for any season!

—David Roth
Founder, Workmatters

Chuck's leadership and mentorship experience really shine in this novel perspective on seasons. Great playbook to prepare for and navigate through the seasonal changes all leaders will encounter.

Lucas Campbell, MD
Chief Transformation Officer,
Washington Regional Medical System

SEASONS
IN LEADERSHIP

A MODEL FOR ADAPTIVE FOCUS, MESSAGE, AND BELIEF

CHUCK HYDE

Seasons in Leadership: A Model for Adaptive Focus, Message, and Belief
© 2023 by Chuck Hyde

All rights reserved. No part of this publication may be reproduced in any form without written permission from Book Villages, P.O. Box 64526, Colorado Springs, CO 80962.

www.bookvillages.com

All Scripture is taken from The ESV® Bible (The Holy Bible, English Standard Version®). ESV® Text Edition: 2016. Copyright © 2001 by Crossway, a publishing ministry of Good News Publishers. The ESV® text has been reproduced in cooperation with and by permission of Good News Publishers. Unauthorized reproduction of this publication is prohibited. All rights reserved.

ISBN-13: 978-1-95756-612-2
Cover and Interior Design by Scot McDonald

LCCN: 2023918296

Printed in the United States of America
1 2 3 4 5 6 7 8 9 10 Printing/Year 27 26 25 24 23

To my wife and sons,
and to our seasons past, present, and future.
I love you dearly.

CONTENTS

Foreword / 9

Preface / 13

Introduction: Situations or Seasons? / 15

Chapter 1: The Model / 19

Chapter 2: External Disruption / 27

Chapter 3: Internal Disruption / 41

Chapter 4: Crisis / 55

Chapter 5: Readiness / 67

Chapter 6: Peak / 79

Chapter 7: Trough / 91

Chapter 8: Acquisition / 103

Chapter 9: Compounding / 119

A Final Thought / 125

Endnotes / 127

Acknowledgments / 133

About the Author / 135

FOREWORD

A little over ten years ago, I transitioned from a long and rewarding military career that included flying helicopters at sea, serving for a number of years as the Director of Leadership Education and Development at the United States Naval Academy and leading a variety of teams and large organizations. Along the way I became an avid student and practitioner of leadership, and, at the time, believed I had a pretty solid understanding and mastery of leadership. And then I met my first "civilian" boss at a coaching and consulting firm in Northwest Arkansas. That boss was Chuck Hyde, who was more than a decade younger than me and from a business background that was about as different as possible from flying high performance military aircraft. But what struck me from my very first meeting with Chuck and challenged my understanding of leadership "mastery" is that we never stop learning and growing, unless we choose to stop. I gained this perspective from Chuck Hyde, who is someone who authentically and deliberately seeks to know himself better and make sense of the world around him.

    It isn't that the humility and curiosity Chuck demonstrated are patently novel. I have long believed that values like humility and curiosity are important. Rather, I learned to challenge my assumptions that humility and curiosity (among other values) are solely the function of wisdom gained from the crucible of experience. Put more simply, I thought that values and wisdom were things to be gained over time and not things actively sought in real-time. Chuck Hyde taught me that the active pursuit of humility and curiosity are not merely an end in itself, but also means to stimulate growth and contribute to success. This helped me see that growth is something we can both experience and direct.

As a student of leadership, I consider myself fortunate to have Chuck Hyde as a teacher, because he continues to challenge and expand my understanding and practice of leadership in his outstanding first book, *Seasons in Leadership*. Here are just a few reasons why you too should place this book on your leadership reading list.

The book begins by defining the concept of "seasons" in organizational leadership. Not unlike a season in nature, a business season is a period of time during which the organization is facing a particular set of challenges and opportunities. While making note that the list is not exhaustive, the book identifies seven very real and important seasons, or sets of challenges and opportunities for most organizations. Through the examples of seasons, the book provides an important lesson in humility for leaders. Many times we avoid or ignore the reality of seasons in organizational life and this book challenges the assumptions that leaders hold around growth and health, the present and future, and the myths and realities of their roles and impact.

Seasons in Leadership is an important read because it provides a framework that is both practical and conceptual, which, for me, makes this book generalizable to so many different leadership and organizational settings and the application of this framework provides important handholds for leaders navigating complex and dynamic circumstances.

The book is also valuable because the concept of "seasons" is not your typical "5 Things or Actions" approach found in so many popular leadership and management texts but an adaptive and relevant way to help leaders make sense, not only of their business and the operating environment, but for powerful insights into the changing nature of their leadership in real-time.

Finally, the book's value is found in the author's real experience leading, coaching and consulting and it's backed up by real-world challenges and learning examples. Chuck Hyde draws on his own experiences, as well as the experiences of his clients, to offer a practical and insightful guide to the seasons of leadership.

Seasons in Leadership is a valuable resource for leaders who seek a different approach to mastery, where leaders both grow in humility and curiosity and are able to navigate the challenges and opportunities of a complex, changing world.

Stephen Trainor, PhD, Captain, USN (ret.)
Professor, Sam M. Walton College of Business, Executive Education, University of Arkansas
Founder, Expeditionary Leadership

PREFACE

In grad school, part of my MBA program had a leadership component to it. In one particular course, the instructor assigned several texts to read. She warned us that the selections would present varying, even divergent, points of view, and that was intentional. She wanted us to wrestle with the broader concept of leadership and the seemingly broader interpretations of what it actually is. In fact, a good deal of time was spent on just trying to define "leadership."

One author we read, a career academic, spent the first 180 pages or so of his book describing why all previous attempts at defining leadership had proven inadequate, with substantial effort given to describing why this was so. Then he decided to unveil the "correct" definition of leadership that he had developed.

I was incredulous. *How arrogant does one have to be, I thought, to spend that much energy shooting holes in others' models and theories only to claim that he (alone) has the insight worthy to develop the correct definition?*

It's been fifteen years since that lecture session, and I still remember the smile on my instructor's face when I went off in class about this author.

Spoiler alert: I don't claim to have an original definition of leadership that refutes others'. In fact, the paper I wrote for that class argued that I think the pursuit of a specific, stand-alone definition of leadership is a bit futile and even a waste of time. Please understand that I've spent the last eighteen years of my professional career directly in the study and application of leadership. Eight of those years, I was CEO of a center for leadership. In the last six years in private practice, I continue to read, listen, and watch the latest in leadership content. I also coach, consult, and write on it. So, I take the topic pretty doggone seriously.

Nonetheless, this is my stated position from grad school that I still hold to today:

I don't know what the definition of leadership is. I just know that people recognize it when they see it. They also recognize when it is absent or poor.

This position is founded on the principle that leadership happens in time and space. In my opinion, it's something to be experienced more than something to be considered. I don't have primary research to support this, and some might find the model I will offer here to be a bit basic ("practical" would be my preferred term). I'm not an academic. I would claim to be a student-practitioner (much like when college sports had student-athletes in the days before Name, Image, and Likeness).

In my consulting practice, I often share with my clients that part of my job is to be constructively provocative. In fact, since you're holding this book, I want to provoke you. Mind you, I don't want to provoke a fight. A synonym with a kinder connotation would be "prompt." But I use "provoke" because I do want to have an edge. I want you to wrestle with these ideas in the same way my grad school instructor provoked me. My hope is that it's on that edge where your senses are sparked, your synapses are firing, and you get super clear on your position on leadership. I hope that the result provokes application in time and space so that your leadership will be clear and compelling to those who are looking for you to lead.

INTRODUCTION

SITUATIONS OR SEASONS?

Situational Leadership Theory, or the Situational Leadership Model, is a model created by Paul Hersey and Ken Blanchard while they were working on *Management of Organizational Behavior*. The theory was first introduced in 1969 as the "life cycle theory of leadership."[1] In the decades since, Situational Leadership (particularly Blanchard's SLII model) has become one of the most talked about, referenced, and recognized leadership models, particularly in that it has proven to have an uncommon enduring quality and relevance. In my coaching practice, I use it frequently in developing leaders as coaches as well as in the context of delegation. Once leaders figure out the imagery of the model, I regularly see the light bulb come on over their head.

To me, the strength of the model juxtaposes a leader's style in the moment with the readiness of the person(s) being led based on their skill and motivation. It fits extraordinarily well at the immediate task or assignment level. While one could argue that the model would hold over a longer time span (and I don't necessarily disagree), my experience has been that it gets applied in relatively short-run situations.

In the fall of 2022, one of my clients began to experience a significant shift in their business climate. Coming off a three- to four-year run of favorable market conditions, the tailwind was now a headwind. The CEO and I had been running a series of workshops for her senior leaders for the prior two years. When we started, it was about equipping the tier just below the executive team with new muscle to handle the volume and the pace of their business, such that leadership would not be a self-limiter to but rather fuel the growth to be had. But all of a sudden, keeping up wasn't the primary concern. When business volume slowed, it became "What do we do *now*?" The idea we began to knock around in planning for this workshop was that while the situation hadn't changed, it was a new *season*, and this season called for a different kind of leadership.

My experience as a coach and consultant is that there is nothing new under sun.[2] Most of what is considered wisdom has already been written, and I think some truths are just timeless. Having said that, context is always changing, so I spend a lot of time and energy paying attention to who's writing and saying what. I call this "the timeliness of the timelessness." Given this, my approach with clients is much like that of a museum curator, bringing forward the best models and thought, and facilitating the "truth" it represents with the client, exploring how that truth best finds application in their circumstances.

As such, I began to research resources regarding this idea of seasonal leadership. Much to my surprise, relatively little is written on this subject, especially when compared to other leadership topics. The one model I found repeatedly in the idea of seasons was that of the calendar year—spring, summer, fall, and winter. Without reading any such source, you could surmise the metaphor: in the spring, things are new, fresh, and emergent; perhaps fragile and needing care. During summer, things are established; conditions are favorable for growth but need attention to not get overexposed. Fall is harvest time, when we reap the rewards of a fully matured "crop" and are posting results. Winter is when things decline. Dormancy may set in. It's cold and not much is growing. In fact, some things may be dying or long dead.

I don't mean to trivialize the validity of this idea or look down my leadership nose at those that would offer it. It's just that in my experience from leading in a Fortune 100 company, as a CEO of a small firm, and now with my consulting clients, this model is just too simple to adequately address the dynamics at play. I'd argue that many leaders would even find such a simplistic model offensive as a representation of their reality. The periodicity and order of four distinct seasons does not map well to the volatility, uncertainty, complexity, ambiguity, and disruption (VUCAD) of the real world.

In my time chairing CEO groups with Vistage Worldwide, we brought in a speaker, Dan Nelson, who told us, "The rate of change will no longer be as slow as it is today." It was a clever twist on an existing idea, but I think it best captures how we have to think about the forces surrounding us as leaders, those that are acting on us and those we might capture for our own leverage. When it comes then to seasons, my hypothesis is that there are more nuanced seasons that demand our attention.

Having found no adequate existing resources, I decided to create my own. I did not consider it too bold as my motive, again, was simply to provoke thought, discussion, and ultimately action for my client. This book is simply the latest iteration of the model born out of that need and the resulting discussion from that group of leaders.

What follows is a dissection of the model and its component parts. We begin by distinguishing seasons from situations and taking a summative look at the factors leaders need to understand, consider, occasionally engineer, and on which they must ultimately act. Beginning in chapter 2, we'll explore exemplary seasons that illustrate the applicability of the model using a historical case study. By no means do I claim that the seasons offered are all-inclusive. Surely, that would prove difficult.

More so, I believe we'd hit a point of diminishing returns. As such, these chapters do not need to be read in consecutive order. Facing external disruption, go to chapter 2. Transitioning to a tough season? Skip to chapter 7.

Taking this one step further, it's my hope that by holding the model up to these cases, it will find utility in the hands of a leader facing a current season, transitioning from one to another, or looking around the corner in anticipation of what's next. Just as leadership style should match readiness of person, so should the leader's readiness, skill, and maturity match the season. Situational awareness and the ability to diagnose are priorities. Whatever the context of the season a leader is facing, the goal is that he or she could overlay the model on the specific contexts and create their own case through application of this structure. If I'm correct that leadership happens in time and space, then the highest value of this book would be its application in untold versions of time and space by leaders across any number of contexts.

In that way, this book is continually being rewritten, with new editions being effectively published with every leader in each new season. Who knows? Maybe this is the start of a crowdsourced movement where iron sharpens iron[3] and leaders co-create new stories of seasons and leadership lived out.

CHAPTER 1

THE MODEL

One morning in early October, I walked into my local Sam's Club. The first aisle of the seasonal section at the front of the store was loaded with Christmas items—wreaths, lights, yard decorations. That wasn't too surprising as the Christmas shopping season has gotten earlier and earlier with each year. What kind of confused me was that the next aisle was dedicated to Halloween—pumpkins, bulk candy, and the like.

I'm a fairly ordered person, so I found it curious that Christmas preceded Halloween for my shopping experience. But what really confused me was that Thanksgiving was nowhere to be found.

What Is a Season?

Seasons take many forms, from holidays to the climate to our favorite sports. Each of us tend to have our favorite seasons and follow suit to take on the spirit of whatever season is current, modifying our behavior and even our mindset accordingly. Fourth of July? Patriotism for Americans. Christmas? Peace on earth and goodwill to men. College football season? Insert your battle cry of choice.

What's particularly interesting about this idea of seasons in leadership is the connectivity to behavior and mindset. If an overweight dude in a red suit can make us feel and act jolly, how much more should we expect the forces of hockey stick growth or a merger of two companies to affect our attitudes and actions in the workplace.

Regardless of its context, most of us can agree on what we mean by a season. Here are at least three things that are true about seasons:

1. They signify or represent a change.
2. There is some duration. And there is an end (that typically begins a new season).
3. They are marked by distinct conditions.

The 1960s rock band The Byrds riffed lyrics from King Solomon in their 1965 classic "Turn! Turn! Turn!":

To everything (turn, turn, turn)
There is a season (turn, turn, turn)
And a time to every purpose under heaven[1]

In my research for this model, one blog post on the topic, written by an army infantry officer with twenty-two years of experience and five deployments to Iraq and Afghanistan, compared the reality of the environment for combat this way: "It's entirely new terrain and it demands adaptation."[2] U.S. history easily points out that the jungle is not the desert, and engaging a sovereign state is different than with a terrorist organization.

A leader's ability to recognize the environment or season and adapt his or her leadership accordingly is paramount to the health and trajectory of the organization and those within. Borrowing further from the military, a common approach to this adaptation is the OODA loop. Developed by U.S. Air Force Colonel John Boyd, the OODA loop represents the sequence employed by pilots in air-to-air combat where OODA stands for observe, orient, decide, and act. This cycle allows one to quickly understand circumstances and make decisions to gain advantage.[3]

Just as Dorothy accurately surmised, "We're not in Kansas anymore," leaders must be able to identify the start of a new season by:

1. Acknowledging the change and defining reality. Leaders must listen, empathize, and remain open to what is happening now and what is likely to happen next.
2. Assessing the risk to the organization and to its people.
3. Creating opportunity. One expression is the equation that New Perspective + New Environment = Growth.
4. Recovering from the previous season. It's possible that at the outset of a new season, it may be necessary to allow for recovery from the preceding season, especially if it was characterized by difficulty or even trauma—hence the term "offseason." The trouble for most of us in organizational life is that there is no offseason.

Five Factors That Demand the Leader's Attention

If seasons are characterized by change, and if leaders are to meet these changes most effectively, it follows that there are specific factors that deserve, *even demand*, attention.

1. **What is this season characterized by?** These are the contextual truths and could include market forces like the economy, competitive activity, customer behavior, emotions, attitudes, and tendencies of our people. Ultimately, this is about what's going on and how we're making sense of it. It deserves calling out that there can be multiple realities at play—this is true *and* this is true *and* . . . Further, there can be differing realities, particularly when it comes to people and how they're making sense of the reality. For example, when considering a crisis situation, there may be some in complete denial while others are nearly paralyzed by fear when faced with the same evidence of what's happening around them.

2. **What should be the organization's focus and activity?** Whatever is true about the forces acting on us, we can choose how we respond—and let's face it, some choices are better than others. By identifying where we should be spending our energy, leaders are effectively establishing the rallying cry that gets everyone on the same page and aligns applied resources accordingly. The choices we force determine resource allocation (where, what, and to what extent), what gets measured and reported, and the like.

3. **What is the leader's role?** In order to align everyone else, the leader must identify, understand, and step into their best role relative to the season. Is it one of being highly directive? Is it that of "chief listener"? Organizational behavior demonstrates repeatedly that those within the organization take their cue from the leaders. Leadership is not an act in terms of fictional theater. However, using the metaphor, if the leader

is the director, everyone—the lead and supporting actors, the stage crew, the makeup artists—is taking their cues from the leader. Therefore, it's essential that leaders consider and choose wisely how they will conduct themselves.

4. **What is the proper tone and message for how and what we communicate?** Study after study demonstrates that people respond as much or more to how information is communicated as compared to the information itself. The channel(s) of communication, its theme, sequence, and frequency all merit intentionality if we stand any chance that those involved will accurately understand what's happening, what's at stake, and what is needed.

5. **What do we want people to believe?** An argument can be made that the preceding four factors all lead to this ultimate fifth factor. People act on beliefs. Attitudes are driven by beliefs. Note, there is an element of marketing here. Think about marketing for a minute. Ads are designed to make us believe something so that we will take action. It seems every third commercial on TV is for insurance. Each will save you money, each will be there when that unfortunate event occurs, and each will greet you with the friendly face of a dude in a red polo, a team dressed in all white with aprons on, or a lovable little gecko. Wireless carriers, another third of all TV ads, are not be outdone. The final third is made up of that piece of exercise equipment that is going to develop ripped abs, the latest blockbuster that is a must-see, and, yes, that book, it's a must-read. Bottom line, shoppers don't act until they believe their decision to buy will

yield their desired result. I believe the same human dynamic is true in organizational life. When I've had leaders I believed in, I would do absolutely what was needed to follow their lead. I've also had a couple of doorknobs in my career that, shall we say, inspired less commitment.

The working hypothesis for this entire book is that these five factors are relevant and can be applied to any season in organizational leadership. No doubt, there are nuances or other ways to dissect seasons. Whether this construct is applied or spurs reflection to new and better thought is not as important as leaders doing the work to understand their season and the resultant action for which it calls.

Seven Seasons

What follows in subsequent chapters is the application of the model on seven representative seasons. Some believe the number seven is the perfect number, representing completeness. This list is far from exhaustive or complete. I chose them only to illustrate common themes from my experience and that of my clients from nearly twenty years of coaching and consulting.

1. **External Disruption**—Change is happening to us.
2. **Internal Disruption**—We are choosing to change.
3. **Crisis**—A special form of external disruption that occurs when stakes are at their highest.
4. **Readiness**—Raw talent abounds, but we are short on experience; the challenge exceeds any reasonable standard of readiness.
5. **Peak**—The wind is at our back, and we are winning on every reasonable level.
6. **Trough**—Headwinds are fierce, and we are losing (or it at least feels that way).

7. **Acquisition**—Change is sparked by two becoming one.

Each chapter walks through the five factors and introduces an exemplary case to illustrate the dynamics at play. Each case presents a dilemma or challenge to be overcome. And spoiler alert, they all end up in a successful outcome, even if it's not always immediate.

It is appropriate and necessary to call out one final dynamic as it relates to the model: seasons often don't operate in isolation. Instead, leaders can easily find themselves in a mix or blend of seasons simultaneously. What happens when External Disruption from a competitor blends with a more macro Crisis (think global pandemic)? Acquisition can be a form of Internal or External Disruption, depending on which side of the table one sits. A start-up, early in its life cycle and in the principals' careers, may be riding the wave of a Peak market. You get the idea.

Because of the likelihood of this occurring at some frequency, treating seasons as stand-alones would be just as inadequate as the spring-summer-fall-winter cycle metaphor that sparked this work. The final chapter considers the leader's dilemma in this season, the compounding effects of the forces acting on the organization, and the multidimensional nature of leadership required.

Let's Get to It

We may debate details, the rationale, and the conclusions, but if in doing so, you have a clearer picture in mind of what seasonal leadership looks like and how you can be a more effective leader, I will have accomplished my objective.

FOR REFLECTION

1. What season have you been in? What season are you currently in? What season do you believe you are headed toward?

2. What's the authentic expression of leadership you need to demonstrate?

3. Reflect on your professional experience. Does a season come to mind that would fit the five factors? What did you believe at that time and why?

CHAPTER 2

EXTERNAL DISRUPTION

In 1998, *Who Moved My Cheese?* by Spencer Johnson hit the shelves and quickly became a bestseller. It remained on the *New York Times* bestseller list for almost five years.[1] It's a simple fable of two mice and two "Littlepeople" in the search for cheese in a maze, and how they react to major change.

My employer at the time distributed copies of the book as instructive allegory to warn of complacency and demonstrate productive and unproductive responses to the inevitability of change. I dutifully read the book and have to confess that while I wasn't crazy about the storyline, I loved the idea and the truths it brought to life regarding change and not getting stuck in your ways.

When I was chairing advisory boards with Vistage Worldwide, I was introduced to what would become one of my favorite exercises: "Disruptor or Disrupted?" In the exercise, a CEO would present his business to the group—everything from financials to org design to strategy and so on. In some cases, the group could even interview key employees and external partners.

We would take that information and split into two smaller groups. One group's assignment was to pick through the data and identify ways they would disrupt the business as a competitor. The other group would use the same information and identify ways the company could play the role of disruptor to its competition and markets. One group was looking for weakness, the other for opportunity.

By having a trusted group of peers outside the organization take these perspectives, the friendly fire often produced meaningful and actionable strategic insight that those within the company might not be able to recognize (read: forest and trees). CEOs that opted in to be the subject of such scrutiny confronted a simple but profound truth: *disruption happens.* The question is really about which side of it you want to be on.

As I sit and write this chapter on a rainy Thursday, I'm four blocks away from the original five-and-dime store where in 1951, Sam Walton opened what would become the world's largest company, Walmart. Less than a mile to my southeast is the company's current world headquarters. A new campus under construction is set to open in 2026 just a mile in the opposite direction. Having grown up in the area and now back as a working executive for the last eighteen years, I often feel as if I have a front-row seat to one of the greatest case studies of entrepreneurialism, competition, and scaling in the history of business.

I've heard the stories from those who lived it and have played roles in select spots. Much of that is attributed to our work at Soderquist Leadership and my relationship to our founding executive, Don Soderquist, retired senior vice chairman and COO at Walmart, who, along with David Glass, were effectively co-successors for Sam Walton when he stepped down.

Don would routinely share his experiences from the company as teaching points to executives who would come to the leadership summits that our firm would host. The stories included Mr. Sam's belief of what was possible in his vision for the company and the hockey stick trajectory its sales numbers would take. One story he would include was a particular newspaper headline that appeared shortly after Walton's death: "Walmart Hits the Wall."

The writer inaccurately asserted the company's success was primarily a force of its founder, and with him gone, the growth could not continue. The results clearly indicate otherwise.

Don would also talk about how the landscape of retailing would change over the decades, where those once in dominant positions—Sears, Kmart, and a bunch of stores you've never heard of—ultimately declined and even went out of business. He asserted that Walmart's secret was its "low RC factor," *RC* meaning "resistance to change."

Walmart's current CEO, Doug McMillon, has been with the company long enough to work under the leadership of Sam, David, and Don, and his other predecessors. This mindset is alive and well under his leadership. One piece of evidence is that he keeps a list of the top ten retailers by decade on his phone as a reminder of the need to innovate, to disrupt or be disrupted.[2]

MBA texts and case studies are full of examples of established market leaders whose proverbial "cheese" was moved by external disruptors.

- The Kodak story (insisting they were a film company when they had the technology for digital imaging in-house) is perhaps the one most oft-cited.

- Streaming media for songs, movies, and TV shows replaced record stores and forever altered movie distributors' and production studios' business models.
- There are few yellow cabs in a ride-share environment.
- Years ago, an executive that attended one of our CEO summits ran a company that manufactured CDs and DVDs—not the content but the discs themselves. And that was it. I remember cringing thinking about the implications of moved cheese.

As we complete our setup of External Disruption, let's be clear that it does not solely come from competition. Look at financial markets and the cost of money in industries like the housing market or in any business's access to the capital it needs for growth. Political election cycles and legislation can alter an industry's landscape (think environment or antitrust acts). Terrorism has proven in recent decades to have massive implications to how we work, travel, and communicate. The final Captain Obvious example would be, I don't know, a global pandemic?

The point I want to make is, again, that disruption happens. When it comes to the disruptive forces acting on us, the question is really about our ability to anticipate and respond, and to bring the rest of our organization with us.

The Model Applied to External Disruption

For the purposes of this examination of External Disruption, I'll approach it from the position of disruption happening *to* us. We take on the "disrupted" title. A season where we seek to be the disruptor deserves separate handling but could be extrapolated from what I hope to show here.

I'll also take the position that the impact of disruption, the bad and the good, may not have happened yet. Signals of potential disruption often come well in advance of any real impact. Others come in the ways that we feel the impact, and it takes some time before we figure out its source. So, we focus on the signal, with or without warning, and the choices available to us in our response.

Finally, I consider disruption to be significant and strategic. This is more than simply a chapter on change. On the spectrum, disruption is on the heavy end. It should not be ignored or underestimated. We aren't simply walking through the change curve. Disruption redefines the game: how it's played, the rules, how the score is kept, and even who is eligible to play. Disruption is a big deal.

What Characterizes External Disruption

Because of the strategic implications that can strike at the core of your organizational model, disruption can quickly feel like an external threat to what you know and even like. It's not at all unusual for this signal that someone wants to shake things up to be met with a range of reactions. On one end, reactions can be characterized by shock and fear that can lead to trying to process what it all means. Self-protection can spark at lots of levels: your company, business unit, location, or career. On the other end, when disruptive signals aren't taken seriously, they can be met with misplaced arrogance and denial.

The response to a signal of External Disruption will be appropriately contextual to the position in which an organization finds itself. One of the most common structural tools of organizational strategy is a SWOT analysis: strengths, weaknesses, opportunities, and threats. I was raised in my career to identify strengths and weaknesses as internal factors and opportunities and threats as external factors. My experience is that a strict adherence to that delineation is helpful in considering a strategic position in such analysis.

External Disruption is then limited to the opportunities or threats it creates. For years, I considered the four components of SWOT as a side-by-side, compare/contrast, four-column list. A far better handling of these four ideas comes from a two-by-two "SWOT matrix."

	OPPORTUNITIES	**THREATS**
STRENGTHS	INVEST Clear matches of strengths and opportunities lead to competitive advantage	DEFEND Areas of threat matched by areas of strength indicate a need to mobilize resources either alone or with others
WEAKNESSES	DECIDE Areas of opportunity matched by areas of weakness require a judgment call: invest or divest; collaborate	DAMAGE CONTROL/ DIVEST Areas of threat matched by areas of weakness indicate need for damage control

Adapted from Kevin P. Kearns, "Comparative Advantage to Damage Control: Clarifying Strategi Issues Using SWOT Analysis." *Nonprofit Management and Leadership 3, no.1 (Fall 1992): 3-22.*

In this model, what's key is the intersection of the external disruption with the internal reality. When dealing with an external threat from a position of strength, entering Defend mode is the natural response. We defend our turf, territory, market share, ways of working, brand, etc. Contrast that with a threat that intersects us at a position of weakness. In essence, there's a threat out there, and we aren't able to defend ourselves. In this case, we enter a mode of Damage Control, potentially divesting, even cutting losses, trying to minimize the impact of things we can't control or influence. (Note: We leave the Opportunities column of the two-by-two matrix for the extrapolating activity of being the "disruptor," ground we'll cover in chapter 3 on Internal Disruption.)

What's key here, and what the two-by-two matrix so effectively points out, is that we need to be aware of our own status in order to properly and most effectively process the disruptive signals that we are experiencing or could conceivably anticipate.

Focus/Activity in External Disruption

Some years ago, Pastor Stuart Briscoe visited the church I attended. In his sermon, he said, "If you take the text out of context, all you're left with is the con." His British accent made the delivery of the quip even more powerful and memorable. So it is when dealing with the threat posed by External Disruption. The intersection of the threat with our position of relative strength or weakness is a major factor in our mindset and prevailing approach in response. Context matters.

Still, you must consider to what degree and in what dimensions the threat exists. It could be an enterprise-level threat that hits every facet of the organization, or it could be much more directed. Consider:

- **Market share.** This is ultimately about volume and your ability to maintain and grow your scale.
- **Reputation.** How does your market perceive your business, whether it is the quality of what is offered or your character and ethics?
- **Cost structures.** If the cost of materials, labor, or other key inputs increases, can that be absorbed in your pricing or did your margin just shrink?
- **Supply chain.** Do you have ready access to what you need in order to do what you do? Are there timing delays or availability issues? Do you need to find alternate sources? Increase your safety stock and inventory footprint?
- **Talent.** Are you able to attract and retain the people you need to operate at your full potential?
- **Brand.** This is about how you are known and what you

are known for. Whether it's premium or value, cutting-edge or archaic, do your customers see you the way you want them to?
- **Channels of delivery**. Can you still distribute, or have consumption patterns changed such that you can't get what you do to your customers the same way?

Clearly, a threat could attack one or more of these dimensions. It bears stating as well that an impact in one dimension could sequentially spill over into others. Therefore, if you are in Defend mode, which fronts need defending? If Damage Control, what holes are you trying to plug to slow the leakage? A methodical, disciplined, and even comprehensive analysis is in order to determine where energy and resources should be deployed.

On July 5, 1994, Jeff Bezos launched Amazon with $10,000 of his own money. I'd argue that few people picked up on the future significance of this disruptive signal. At that time, books were sold in stores with shelves and chairs and coffee shops. In addition to books, these stores also sold highlighters, pens, bookmarks, and book lights. Thinking back on it, it almost feels like stone tablets and hieroglyphics.

Here are just a few other key dates in the Amazon trajectory:

- 1998 – Expands beyond books
- 2005 – Launches Amazon Prime
- 2006 – Launches Amazon Kindle
- 2007 – Launches Amazon Fresh
- 2008 – Acquires Audible
- 2010 – Kindle e-books outsell hardcover books on Amazon by almost 50 percent
- 2017 – Acquires Whole Foods
- 2018 - $1 trillion market cap reached
- 2022 – Acquires MGM[3]

One could argue that Amazon is the single biggest disruptor in the last quarter century, if not in all of human history, depending on your metric. This is particularly true if you throw in all of the fast followers that Amazon aided by simply demonstrating what could be done with production and consumption of content, retail sales, and all the derivatives. In the last twenty or so years, Amazon has been on an unrelenting quest to put smiles on our faces with everything from A to Z (just look at their logo).

Coming back to our friends down the street at Walmart, much of what the traditional shopper experience had been was threatened to be sure. People outside the company were again predicting Walmart's demise. In 2015, Walmart suffered its first year-on-year sales decrease since 1970.[4] Walmart had been experimenting with e-commerce for some time but doubled down when it purchased Jet.com in 2016. In 2017, it acquired online retailers Bonobos and Moosejaw as well as logistics company Parcel, which specialized in last-mile delivery.[5]

Referring back to the two-by-two SWOT matrix, Amazon was a real threat to Walmart's strength, and the company went into Defend mode. Still, many prognosticators felt it would be too little, too late. To them, Walmart was done as the dominant force in retail.

Borrowing from ESPN football analyst Lee Corso, "Not so fast, my friend." This case study is still being written. Unexpectedly, Walmart began to flip the script on its new rival. To this point, Walmart's physical store footprint had been characterized as a weakness, both on the balance sheet and as an operating model—that is, until they were recognized as de facto distribution centers. These weren't distribution centers in excess of one million square feet strategically located on major highways and in population centers several hundred miles apart. Not at all. Walmart's footprint put 90 percent of the U.S. population within ten miles of a store.[6] Former JC Penney CEO Ron Johnson noted, "The huge storage and shelf space in the typical Walmart store actually allows inventory to be 'forward deployed' to where the customer is, 'an advantage that is hard to beat.'"[7] All of a sudden, Amazon had a distribution and cost-of-delivery threat on its radar, exposing a weakness. "Uh . . . let's buy Whole Foods." One might argue the two-by-two SWOT matrix breaks down here. Is that Damage Control or Investment? I'd argue the former, but in this high-stakes game of chess, Walmart put its disrupted hat to the side and donned that of a disruptor, using infrastructure it already had as its base to grow its pickup and delivery business, forcing a response from Amazon.

In a 2019 article, Moody's lead retail analyst Charlie O'Shea noted, "Walmart has nailed the [question of]: 'How do we transition online?' Now, they aren't building stores, but are spending about the same on capex . . . that's going into technology spend and going into e-commerce." In the same article, Liz Dunn, founder and CEO of Pro4ma, a forecasting tool for retailers, said, "Long term, [Walmart] is using its size to go head-to-head against Amazon. And it's working."[8]

The Leader's Role in External Disruption

Given the strategic nature of disruptive threats, it follows that the leader's role is that of a strategist. It's worth noting that this should not fall on that individual alone, as a prudent leader seeks relevant input from trusted sources. Still, strategy is what's in demand.

Tom Verdery, a Procter & Gamble executive, joined our team at Soderquist Leadership upon his retirement as executive-in-residence and was responsible for leading our strategic planning efforts. I don't know if it was original to him, but one of the things he taught me was that strategies are the choices you force. Effectively, a choice to do one thing, by definition, is a choice not to do something else. In disruption, choice making is critical to the organization's forward trajectory, and the leader is the chief choice maker.

Consider this quote from Doug McMillon on its acquisitions related to e-commerce in our working case study:

> The acquisitions have received a lot of attention, but our plan in e-commerce is not to buy our way to success. The majority of our growth is and will be organic. The acquisitions are helping us speed some things up. So overall, we're making progress in providing the seamless shopping experience our [customers] desire and we will keep moving along this journey.[9]

McMillon is on record that Walmart wants a "repetitive" relationship with its shoppers, a core fundamental of this strategy and one that appears to be working. "We've shared before—if people buy in-store and online with Walmart.com, they generally spend twice as much and they shop in-store more often."[10]

The Tone and Message in External Disruption

As established at the outset of the chapter, External Disruption first occurs at the signal that it exists, with or without impact. "Attention!" is the message with External Disruption. We don't want to miss the signal. Something has introduced itself so that business as usual is, at least potentially, no longer usual. Tone might vary depending on the immediacy and severity of impact. It might well be a shout. It's conceivable that a more polite approach makes sense. "Ladies and gentlemen, may I have your attention for a moment? I'm so very sorry for the interruption."

My experience suggests that if the threat is real, it's better to err on the side of urgency and intensity. Wherever one lands on the continuum, the call for attention needs to be effective.

Belief in External Disruption

Central to response to any form of External Disruption is

the leader's ability to get people to believe the threat is real. Some in the organization may already get it, but it is a positive thing if they know their leader knows it. This isn't about lack of confidence. It's about "I see it, and we will respond."

On the other end of the spectrum, those who are skeptical, in denial, or mired in a false sense of security and misplaced arrogance have to come along. A leader can be the chief strategist and the chief executive, but he needs his people to come along to get things done. The best answers to the threat may be within the rank and file, and the leader needs access to those answers. Even if there is a push "down" through the organization of what the strategic response will be, people have to buy in for it to be fully effective. If they don't believe the threat is real, they might simply go through the motions, complying with the expectations set at a minimal level. In contrast, if they believe, they will commit themselves, all of themselves, to the response plan.

FOR REFLECTION

1. Do you and your leadership team possess credibility in the eyes of your people to get them to believe in your ability to respond to External Disruption? If not, what should you be doing now to build that?

2. Have you considered the SWOT analysis as a two-by-two matrix, looking at the intersections of internal strengths and weaknesses against external opportunities and threats?

3. If your competitors wanted to disrupt you, what would they do? Do you have people close to you that would give you the friendly fire to help you see potential blind spots?

4. If your business wanted to be a disruptor in your sector, what could you do? Do you have people close to you that could show you things in your forest that you can't see because of all the trees?

5. Do you have an appropriate level of productive paranoia that allows you to anticipate External Disruption and detect early signals so you can respond to your best advantage and outcome?

CHAPTER 3

INTERNAL DISRUPTION

In December 1992, I graduated from the University of Arkansas with a degree in chemical engineering. Earlier in that semester, I had told my best friend that I'd had my first interview with what would be my future employer, Kimberly-Clark Corporation (K-C), to which he inquired, "Was she nice?"

That's kind of funny, and if you knew my friend, you'd probably just roll your eyes, but in the coming years I always had to qualify who I worked for with some version of "You know their brands: Kleenex, Huggies, Depend, Kotex." The quizzical looks would change to "Oh, got it." My twelve years at K-C were entirely in the personal-care products supporting the feminine, adult, and baby-care businesses. As an integrated company, I also got a lot of firsthand exposure to our nonwovens business and pulp mills.

At that time, K-C was pretty diversified in its holdings. The nonwovens business supplied our personal-care businesses with raw materials in addition to selling on the open market. It was also a strategic competitive supplier to our professional health-care business. I often tell people, open up a supply closet in any hospital in the country, and you're bound to see a ton of K-C products in surgical masks, gowns, sheets, etc.

As a paper company, we had our own pulp mills. I got to

visit one in Coosa Pines, Alabama, and was struck by the image of a truck of pine trunks that I'd seen on the highway. I distinctly remember a big crane with jaws that could take those logs in one chomp and deposit them on a pile so big they looked like matchsticks.

A company with an integrated supply chain really isn't that uncommon. Again, it gave us a competitive edge in product development and shelterable technology but also in our supply chain. What was a little less expected is that we had our own trucking company. One could argue this was just another form of integration in hauling our own product. Sure, but it wasn't dedicated, and we still had plenty of other haulers.

What about an airline? K-C owned Milwaukee-based Midwest Express Airlines, where every seat was a first-class seat, real meals were served, and they baked chocolate-chip cookies *on board* every flight (yes, you could smell them in the oven and had to make sure you didn't get melted chocolate all over your business attire).

Fast-forward a few years, and Jim Collins released his iconic

Good to Great in 2001. I was then working in the diaper business at our headquarters in Neenah, Wisconsin. The book was quite the buzz, and K-C was among the fifteen featured companies that Collins had studied. He credited CEO Darwin Smith for leading the transformation from K-C being a paper company to a consumer products company. Smith retired in 1991, so I never got to sit under his leadership. I can say that a number of company veterans I worked with early in my career who had seen Smith in action thought he hung the moon.

Wayne Sanders succeeded Smith as CEO and carried on the remaining parts of the plan of company makeover initiated by Smith, selling the pulp mills, the paper company, the trucking company, and the airline. Exiting those businesses allowed the company to refocus its investments into its consumer brands. I had a front-row seat for that as a young leader, by then leading capital projects in our Huggies business.

It was reassuring to feel like we had a plan. Granted, I was in the most profitable business in the company at the time and could feel the swell of support we were getting. Clearly, I was on the right side of that Internal Disruption. I also had access to the "why" behind the moves and understood how we planned to win in this new era of the company—and I really liked knowing how we were going to win.

While this is not the place to dissect the various moves by the company in this period, it is a terrific case of understanding that by saying "no" to one thing, it allows one to say "yes" to something else. The company saw many of these assets as nonstrategic. Most can probably see that was true of the airline, but even the pulp mills, while producing a key raw material in absorbent products, became nonstrategic. Yes, we'd still use pulp, but we didn't need to own the pulp mills that were capital intensive and producing a commodity.

Zooming way out, this was all about becoming a company that investors saw differently. Instead of being compared with a peer group of International Paper and Georgia-Pacific, K-C wanted its peer group to be Unilever, Procter & Gamble, and Colgate-Palmolive—and in doing so, it became great.

The Model Applied to Internal Disruption

While I admittedly struggle with the definition of leadership, one of my favorites is that leadership is the ability to get people to want to do the thing you're absolutely convinced should be done. Jim Collins's assertion is that "good is the enemy of great."[1] It follows that if things are good, it might be a bit of a challenge to get people to *want* to disrupt that. Internal Disruption is just that—a decision to change, at times when things are good because you believe great is a possibility.

What Characterizes Internal Disruption

"Why?"

This isn't as simple as a toddler repeatedly trying to understand their need to comply with a parental direction or how the universe works. It is still arguably *the question* that would characterize reactions to Internal Disruption. After all, if things are going reasonably well, why should we self-inflict change? We've heard (and likely said) it all before:

- If it ain't broke, don't fix it.
- Don't mess with a good thing.
- You don't know what you got until it's gone.

Questioning is the central theme of Internal Disruption. Even for those who are forward-thinking enough to be comfortable with the "why" of change, its cousins are quick to follow: Who? What? Where? How? In some ways, people are interested and have a genuine desire to know. Others may have their own ideas and want to create debate among the available choices. Questions aren't a bad thing. Great debate can spur on great decisions. The debate is a necessary and expected component of Internal Disruption.

To some degree, leaders can expect a certain amount of questioning the need to change. Salespeople call this "overcoming the status quo bias," where they have to overcome the prospect's latent desire to do anything different from what they're already doing. There are potential layers to this. The first, we've already pointed out—if things are going well, why would we change at all?

There is another layer that can be even more difficult to overcome, and that is any form of protectionism that would fight against displacement of something we know and do well. It's noteworthy that for many, any form of change represents loss. This could be a loss of something they hold dear—a process or a product, for example, especially if they helped create it. Another potential form of loss is that of identity, in the nature of their job or the job itself. Still another is a more general loss of "it's just not like how it used to be," which is more emotional than logical.

It's this component that leaders must be able to answer if they're going to get people to want to do the thing the leaders are convinced should be done.

Focus/Activity in Internal Disruption

One of my favorite models around Internal Disruption is the sigmoid curve. A sigmoid curve is simply a mathematical function that takes the shape of an S. Organizational psychologist Charles Handy is credited with transferring this mathematical function to change theory.[2] In short, if a company's growth is headed up and to the right as we would hope over time, the trick is knowing when to jump to a new curve before the current one hits maturity, levels off, and ultimately goes into decline.

Short term, the performance is likely to drop until a new mastery occurs and growth resumes that surpasses the former paradigm and what it could have produced. This new curve should inevitably, in turn, be replaced by a subsequent curve, and so on. The trick is twofold:

- Timing the jump.
- Having the courage to make it.

In employing this model, the focus and activity should be about the new curve and the jump that the organization needs

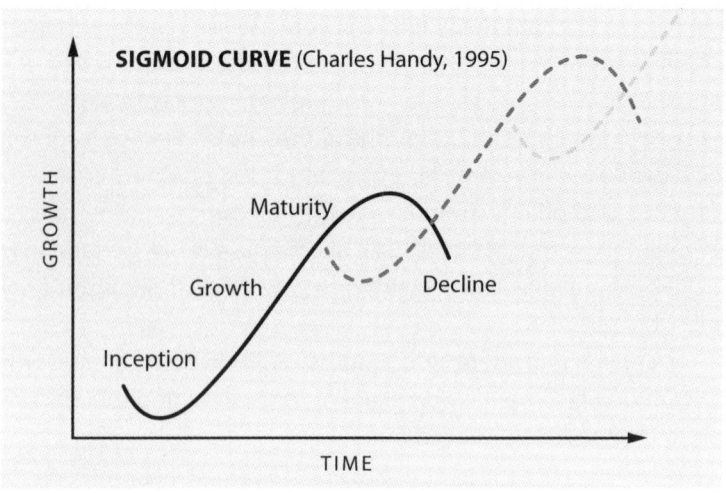

to make. Once you have answered "why," this is about defining the new curve. People will work most effectively when provided with clarity about the new direction, what's expected, and what others are counting on them to deliver, both at the end and in the transition. This includes the preparatory work of getting ready to make the jump as well as what to expect once the new curve is the norm. Most of us, when provided with that clarity, can get on board with where the leader is convinced we need to go.

The Leader's Role in Internal Disruption

During that same season inside K-C's diaper business, I was privileged to be part of a corporate team selected to study General Electric's Change Acceleration Process (CAP). This group had the opportunity to travel to Crotonville, New York, to visit GE's internal leadership development campus where we met with GE corporate leaders entrusted with CAP and its leadership initiatives. It was fascinating and pretty weighty stuff. I can't say that I'd sign up for everything GE promoted, and I'm not a big Jack Welch fan, but I recall thinking CAP had a lot of merit.

Back at the K-C home office, we began to internalize how we'd drive change in the company and to socialize these four roles when it came to driving internal change:

- **The Change Sponsor.** This role typically occurs at the executive level and is the person who effectively commissions the change activity. This is often the answer to the question, "Says who?" (Um, the CEO.) The sponsor's role is about providing broad endorsement and the big picture. They are the one to secure and provide adequate resources, and they are often the one describing what success looks like at the end state.
- **The Change Leader.** This role is typically the agent of the sponsor (if not actually the same person). This

person is ultimately responsible for the outcome and the activities that are designed to produce it. They are tracking, directing, and at times even interpreting.
- **The Change Manager.** This might be the most difficult of the roles in that this is the leverage point of where change happens, at the executional level. Change managers manage resources and processes, monitoring and reporting on whether things are taking effect. They are the direct contact to the rest of the organization in enrolling their commitment to what's being asked.
- **Change Agents.** These are people within the organization, often without positional authority, who are leverage points for the organization to push through and/or accelerate change. This could be about the role they play, their skill set, or their personal credibility among the ranks—or any combination thereof. Identifying and enrolling change agents early multiplies leadership and the message we need to send.

Perhaps the preeminent voice on change is Harvard professor John Kotter. He called this element "creating the guiding coalition," which includes position power, expertise, credibility, and leadership.[3] The key lesson here is that the leader needs other leaders to step into these roles. Internal Disruption, *especially* if it's strategic, requires multiple people in these various roles if the change is to be effective and sustainable.

The Tone and Message in Internal Disruption

On September 12, 1962, at Rice University, President John F. Kennedy gave his first speech on going to the moon. Kennedy was inspirational in this iconic presidential moment. Many argue that it is the best example of setting vision—something that's both inspirational and aspirational, that describes a new state, and that you have no idea on how you're going to achieve it.

Kennedy's words, "we choose to go to the moon," painted a picture of America's shared future. Clearly the context of the Space Race and the Cold War with the Soviets provided plenty of motivation and alignment.

> We choose to go to the moon in this decade and do the other things, not because they are easy, but because they are hard; because that goal will serve to organize and measure the best of our energies and skills, because that challenge is one we are willing to accept, one we are unwilling to postpone, and one we intend to win, and the others, too.[4]

There are two interesting subplots around Kennedy's address at Rice University. First, it wasn't the first time Kennedy had cast this vision. Indeed, on May 25, 1961, Kennedy stood before Congress and called for this same audacious move. However, a Gallup poll indicated that 58 percent of Americans opposed the idea.[5]

The second is that while Kennedy's speech focused on going to the moon and is remembered for that, he was simultaneously setting the stage for a much bigger idea for America's leadership. Going to the moon was just the next example, the next sigmoid curve. If we listen closely, Kennedy is also saying there are subsequent curves we'll jump to next.

Make no mistake, painting a picture of our shared vision is essential to bridging people into the "want to" category of disruption and is the central tone and message of Internal Disruption. My former boss and mentor Don Soderquist often said there was a difference between compliance and commitment. Compliance gets people to go along and meet expectations at the most. Commitment, on the other hand, gets people excited and gives discretionary effort to meet their future. It answers WIIFM? (What's in it for me?) for anyone who needs it. When we emotionally and logically connect others to our *shared* future state, we all have a reason to grab an oar and start rowing.

Belief in Internal Disruption

The outcome of all this effort is the belief that we want to. I had an old football coach who challenged our team one day after practice, "Who here wants to win?" As you might expect, everyone raised their hand. What he followed with has stuck with me nearly forty years later: "Who here wants to *do what it takes* to win?" It's a brilliantly subtle and substantial difference. I saw it in my not-so-spectacular athletic career and in my professional career as well.

As leaders, when we can get people to believe that they want to do the thing we're absolutely convinced should be done, they're willing to do what it takes to make the jump, to endure the short-term blip for the long-term gain.

Final Touches

In my time as CEO at Soderquist Leadership, we were attempting a significant disruption that was internally driven. We were experiencing many of the same questions around "why," and I brought in an external facilitator to help us navigate our path. He introduced me to my favorite graphic on change, and it's from the book *The Change Monster*.[6] This image is worth the study. Look at the y-axis of Morale & Confidence as well as the five phases along the x-axis beginning with Stagnation and ending with Fruition. Consider the terrain changes, the obstacles that must be overcome, and the pivot points along the way.

In this particular season of Internal Disruption at our center, I used this image with our team very early on in the process, asking each person to plot independently where they thought we were on this curve. As you might expect, there was a cluster of votes very early along the path, mostly in the Preparation stage. A few leaders who had a much clearer view had progressed toward

INTERNAL DISRUPTION

CHANGE CURVE

[Figure: Change Curve diagram showing the phases Stagnation → Preparation → Implementation → Determination → Fruition, with Morale & Confidence on the y-axis. Key markers along the curve include: "Organization is depressed or hyperactive" (Stagnation); "Decision to Change is Made," "Appetite for Change Reaches Critical Mass," "Leaders Engage in Planning & Communication," "Vision, Strategy & Plan are Shared" (Preparation); "Awareness that Something is Wrong," "Initiative Involves More People in Multiple Layers" (Implementation); "Crisis," "Conflicts, Clashes, Failures & Minor Successes" (Determination); "Change is Abandoned" off-ramp, "Results are Realized" (Fruition).]

the early stages of Implementation. A couple of outliers stood out. There were a few dots to the left of Decision to Change Is Made. Clearly, I had not communicated effectively with these team members. But more unexpectedly, one vote was all the way to Fruition. I thought, *Wow! What's that about?* The exercise, while not statistically valid, did give me a temperature of the room and our leadership team a sense of what we needed to do to continue to enroll our team in our case of Internal Disruption.

Some months later, well down the road, I decided it was time to take our temperature once again and asked everyone to plot on the graph where they thought we were in the change now. Again, the spread was telling. In actuality, we were probably somewhere close to the option to take the off-ramp to Change Is Abandoned. There was a sizable cluster around the Crisis bomb and definitely some stragglers in the Preparation and Implementation phases. This was not about a specific determinant of status. It was about where people *believed* we were.

This new distribution told our leadership team two things: we had indeed made progress, but we were farther spread in how we saw it collectively. It would have been easy to be discouraged that people didn't see us farther on the path than they did, but

I didn't see it that way. To me, it clearly informed that we had much work to do to pull people through the change, so we went back our message.

Ultimately, this experience demonstrated the iterative and repetitive nature of leading in Internal Disruption. As leaders, we can't give a "We Choose to Go to the Moon" speech and expect everyone to just get it. It's a repeat loop of a playlist that helps the early adopter remain clear and the skeptic understand that we're serious.

FOR REFLECTION

1. Where do you land on your current sigmoid curve? Are you still on the upslope? Cresting? Headed downhill?

2. What compelling story of your shared future have you shared recently with your people? Have you given them a reason to want to go there with you?

3. Who are the change agents in your organization that you can count on to help bring other people along? How are you purposefully investing in them? How are you positioning them to bring others along?

CHAPTER 4

CRISIS

From September 7, 1940, to May 11, 1941, roughly 150 Nazi air raids, known as The Blitz, dropped over 30,000 tons of bombs on British targets. At the outset, London was bombed fifty-six of the first fifty-seven days and nights of this campaign.[1] Winston Churchill had been an underwhelming politician early in his career, not taken seriously within Parliament for most of his service. Yet in 1940, he was appointed to succeed Neville Chamberlain as British prime minister. Chamberlain's leadership had failed on several levels. He was among those leaders in power in Europe who discounted the threat of a young Adolf Hitler rising in political power in Germany, dismissing the possibility that he could pose a problem for Germany, much less Europe, the rest of the world, and an entire people group. In contrast, it was Churchill who had the foresight to see the threat Hitler posed, despite no one's willingness to listen.

In a 1935 essay, Churchill wrote, "If . . . we look only at the past, which is all we have to go by, we must indeed feel anxious. Hitherto, Hitler's triumphant career has been borne onwards, not only by a passionate love for Germany, but by currents of hatred so intense as to sear the souls of those who swim upon them."[2]

By 1940, England's prospect of withstanding the Nazi onslaught was not good. The country was on the brink of surrender, and some British leaders were considering that eventuality. Yet, Churchill, now freshly appointed as prime minister, was told by an adviser on the drive from Buckingham Palace, "You have an enormous task"; the most immediate was the extraction of 340,000 soldiers pinned down against Nazi forces at Dunkirk, across the English Channel on the French coast.[3] In his first public address as prime minister, Churchill clearly stated his position regarding the war:

> We have before us an ordeal of the most grievous kind. We have before us many, many months of struggle and suffering. . . . You ask, what is our aim? I can answer in one word: It is victory, victory at all costs, victory in spite of all terrors, victory, however long and hard the road may be; for without victory, there is no survival.[4]

Later that year, Churchill reaffirmed his resolve in his "We Shall Fight on the Beaches" speech to the House of Commons:

> We shall go on to the end, we shall fight in France, we shall fight on the seas and oceans, we shall fight with growing confidence and growing strength in the air, we shall defend our Island, whatever the cost may be, we shall fight on the beaches, we shall fight on the landing grounds, we shall fight in the fields and in the streets, we shall fight in the hills; we shall never surrender![5]

Again, in October 1941, in a speech to Harrow, his alma mater, he tripled down:

> You cannot tell from appearances how things will go. Sometimes imagination makes things out far worse than they are; yet without imagination not much can be done. Those people who are imaginative see many more dangers than perhaps exist; certainly many more than will happen; but

then they must also pray to be given that extra courage to carry this far-reaching imagination. But for everyone, surely, what we have gone through in this period—I am addressing myself to the School—surely from this period of ten months this is the lesson: never give in, never give in, never, never, never, never—in nothing, great or small, large or petty—never give in except to convictions of honour and good sense. Never yield to force; never yield to the apparently overwhelming might of the enemy.[6]

As Americans, we largely don't know what it means to fight a war on our own soil. Other than the attacks on Pearl Harbor and the terrorist acts of 9/11, we don't know what it means to see devastation in such a deep and close way, and certainly not over a prolonged period of time.

That is a sharp contrast to what our British allies understood, particularly for World War II. The Nazi attacks on Britain were absolutely devastating as Hitler sought to have England succumb just as the rest of Europe had. What Churchill understood politically, to mirror what he understood militarily, was that there was a war to be fought in the minds of the British citizenry. He needed them to believe.

Indeed, noted writer and member of Parliament A. P. Herbert commented a Churchill speech "was like an organ filling the church, and we all went out refreshed and resolute to do or die." Across the Atlantic, little is recorded regarding President Franklin D. Roosevelt's reactions to Churchill's wartime broadcasts. First Lady Eleanor Roosevelt, however, said Churchill's speeches "were a tonic to us here in the United States as well as to his own people."[7]

The Model Applied to Crisis

What we've learned through neuroscience is that when emotions are running high, it is difficult for us to think clearly. I've had people describe being in a fog when it's hard simply to process. Others will describe being stuck, effectively paralyzed in their inability to process information or think rationally through circumstance. Crisis can bring this on. And guess what? Leaders aren't immune to this.

People default to a position that the leader is supposed to know what's going on—what brought this about and, more importantly, exactly how we're going to get out of it. While it may not be exactly fair (welcome to leadership), it is understandable that it would be helpful to have a construct to put into play, making sense of things so that we can help others do the same.

What Characterizes Crisis

Imagine a lighthouse. What do you see? I'm not talking about one of those chamber-of-commerce days when it is warm, sunny, a breeze powering the sailboats just out from shore. Nah, I'm talking about a storm. Maybe even the perfect storm. You see it, don't you? Waves crashing on the rocks. Torrential rain falling at a diagonal. The darkness penetrated only by the flashes of lightning. And one small light, rotating in a circular fashion. The lighthouse.

In my time at Soderquist Leadership, one of our core models for leadership was that of a lighthouse. We would posit that the core purposes of lighthouses were to (1) serve as a reference point and (2) show the way of safe passage. In this model, we would contend that on peaceful days, the lighthouse, while arguably working, wasn't adding a lot of essential value. If it was not working or even was absent, those on the water would have clear visibility to understand where they were and would be able to navigate their course safely.

Not so with the storm. In those moments, the lighthouse had to be present and operational. In the days before GPS and all that goes with it, ship captains depended on the lighthouse to be that constant point of reference for navigation, warning of danger and showing safe passage.

So it is with leadership. There are plenty of seasons when people within an organization have clarity, the threat level is relatively low, and they can figure things out on their own. But in Crisis, in the storm, those same people are looking for the leader. They're looking for that consistent point of reference that they can bank on to help inform their actions and decisions, and while things may be really rough, they have a certain peace that everything is going to work out.

Carrying out this characterization of Crisis past the circumstances, we should think about what's going on with our people—the sailors, as it were. Crisis can bring about uncertainty, anxiety, stress, or difficulty coping. "We know our jobs, but we weren't trained for *this*." It's the "this" that brings about the anxiety, whether real or perceived. And here's the thing: they might be right. Maybe we never really could have anticipated the possibility of a given crisis (see global pandemic). Still here we are. The context is real, and how people are processing it is every bit as real.

Focus/Activity in Crisis

In chapter 2, we introduced a model for a SWOT matrix. In Crisis, we can invoke this to begin to frame how we think about a crisis. Whatever the threat to our organization, are we experiencing it from a position of strength? If so, then it's about *defending* our position. If the threat is exposing a weakness, it's about *damage control*. In this construct, Crisis is simply (if you can say simply) an extreme case of External Disruption. This isn't meant to downplay Crisis. It is its own season for a reason. When you've been in Crisis, you know this to be true.

Several years ago, I found myself in the midst of a struggle that I believed fit the criteria of Crisis. In this particular situation, I'm not sure whether my team fully understood the depth of the crisis. That was OK at the time. There are times when the leader identifies something, through experience and/or having more access to information, before the rest of the crew. I recall vividly a family weekend at my parents' house and being called out by one of my siblings for being checked out all weekend. I was guilty as charged. I hadn't shared what was going on at work. I wasn't trying to be a bad son, brother, uncle, husband, or dad. I was, however, pretty consumed by the crisis.

I happened to be reading *Seven Lessons for Leading in Crisis* by Bill George.[8] It had been previously recommended to me, and given the situation, I could take all the lessons I could get. The one "aha" experience I recall from somewhere in the middle of that text was that the worst time to start reading about leading in a crisis is when you're already in one.

Still, I found it to be a wonderfully helpful resource that I highly recommend. It makes little sense to repeat George's work here. I suggest you buy and read the book. In reviewing the book, as telling as George's wisdom were my personal notes that I journaled in the margins and at the end of each chapter:

> ~ *What evidence do I have that makes me believe what I think is important and effective actually is?*
>
> ~ *How do I frame the crisis for the extended team to get the right/needed response?*
>
> ~ *Fear of letting others down plus arrogance that I'm actually capable of pulling it off.*
>
> ~ *Who do I have available to me?*
>
> ~ *What are the root causes for the problems we're facing right now? How did we get here?*
>
> ~ *Normal will be different. Accept it, anticipate it, act on it.*
>
> ~ *How can we use this to trigger our future?*

Looking back nearly fifteen years later, the exercise of reading George's book and, more importantly, the reflection it prompted were about trying to find focus and determine what we should be doing in the midst of the crisis that no one saw coming.

To this point, we've kind of assumed that we couldn't have seen a crisis coming and that we were completely unprepared, but that isn't always the case. Sailors may have the weather forecast. At sea, one can see a storm from miles away. And certainly, training and equipment can be put in place for readiness when, not if, a storm comes. In these crises, the focus and activity can be effectively executing our crisis response plan.

In 2003, I was taking a career transfer at Kimberly-Clark to what at that time was the company's largest U.S. facility. I was not the plant manager but on the plant management team and, as such, would at times be asked to serve as acting plant manager whenever he was unavailable.

We had a crisis management manual—a red three-inch, three-ring binder. The binder's tabs flagged the various crises that we could conceivably encounter. I don't recall all the tabs, but I'm sure it would have included severe weather/acts of God, perhaps an active shooter situation, or even catastrophic equipment failure. The steps under each tab would have included the immediate threat, notification of authorities, notification of corporate resources, handling the media, etc. It was our playbook, and while we weren't expected to memorize its details, we were expected to know how to execute flawlessly and consistently with the company's expectations. The lesson here is that crisis management has a lot to do with the forethought, planning, and resource deployment that are all in place because leaders are *prepared*.

Several years ago, I met and became friends with Major General Harold L. Timboe, United States Army (Retired). He also is a medical doctor. He had recently relocated back to Northwest Arkansas. I knew two of his adult children. It was his daughter who reached out and suggested we meet. Somewhere along the way, I was given his bio. It was jaw dropping and included leading army medicine, leading a term at Walter Reed Medical Center, and accumulating many experiences in mass casualty situations, not something he sought but rather that just came his way. I remember thinking, *I never really thought about it, but I'm glad someone has that specialty, I guess.*

On the way to our first meeting, I called his daughter and asked, "What do I call him? General? Doctor? Doctor General?" I distinctly remember her response: "I don't know. We just call him Dad." That told me a lot about the leader I was about to meet.

In time, Dr. Timboe (it's Harold, he insists) relayed a number of stories—from his days at West Point that overlapped with a basketball coach named Bobby Knight to his active-duty experiences. One such story particularly stood out.

We all remember where we were on September 11, 2001. Timboe was leading the crisis response at the Pentagon after terrorists flew a plane into its southwest wall. In recounting how his team led in that scene, he simply characterized it as "we executed our plan." As it turns out, not long before the attack, they had run a drill on just such an emergency. The dry run exposed a number of areas that needed to be better. With those addressed, when the drill became live, they were indeed prepared and executed extraordinarily well in the most extraordinary of circumstances, minimizing casualties and damages. We can't know who or what was effectively saved by this level of readiness. What is clear, though, is the focus and activity for everyone involved were well defined, well prepared for, and well carried out.

In my conversation with Harold leading up to this chapter, he offered the following from his career experiences:

> As a synopsis for this kind of preparedness, it is essential for organizations and their leaders that might be susceptible to various scenarios of catastrophes, and their subordinate

units and leaders, to know all their missions and what their higher authorities expect of their response capabilities. You might summarize it in these four broad capability areas:

- Know your vulnerable scenarios and have a plan for responding to each. The plan relies on the mix of people and their specialty capabilities required to respond to the situation.
- The people and leaders rely on the variety and amounts of products mix available to get the situation under control, including communication, an operations center for coordination and keeping track of execution, and evacuation of the most critically injured people from the predesignated casualty collection points.
- There needs to be a capability plan for rapid resupply of the right mix of products to the points they are needed.
- And key to making this all work efficiently is practice, practice, practice, especially for the leaders getting all of this rolling and giving wise directions. After each practice of a scenario, it is important to have an assembly of leaders and certain staff to learn from the critique/after-action review.

Units and leaders benefit immensely from these types of exercises, gaining familiarity and confidence. In summary, this is Plans, People, Products, Practice (rehearsal). It worked for me many times, and my higher authorities breathed a sigh of relief when an event happened and they realized everything was in place to execute the mission at hand.

The Leader's Role in Crisis

Whether in military contexts or in business, timing during a Crisis is urgent and stakes are high. Given this, the leader's role becomes that of a director. No doubt, deputies have roles, but they converge to and emanate from a central point or command center. The director ensures things are in sync and in proper sequence. The right information is flowing to the right people in the right channels. Nothing more, nothing less. There is little to no time for consensus building, so decisions become much more autocratic, even for a consensus-building leader.

And they must. In the instances when plans are in place, direction is about running the play. If those plans don't exist, then the director must ensure the right inputs are being secured, made sense of, and then acted upon. There may be more than one cook in the kitchen, but the leader must understand there can only be one executive chef calling the shots.

The Tone and Message in Crisis

Perhaps more than any other season, Crisis will be chaotic and noisy. Information is flowing fast, and the volume is loud from every direction. It's in these details that leaders must make sense of what's happening and what's at stake at any given front in order to make decisions. Information tends to change a lot in crisis and at times even be seemingly contradictory. What we thought we were certain of just a moment ago has now been rendered invalid.

Because of extreme dynamics at play, the tone and message in Crisis are a call to arms. Every person, every resource is in motion or at the ready. No one is sitting this out. When done well, it will be a harmonious blend of people stepping up and into their defined roles while others may be asked to step up and *out of* their defined roles, contributing wherever and however is asked. The crisis is shared, as is everyone's individual and collective interests.

Belief in Crisis

In Crisis, a leader needs people to believe "We will prevail." If we applied a common contemporary marketing tactic, that might show up as "WE. WILL. PREVAIL." If our hypothesis is correct, that people's attitudes and actions will be shaped and influenced by what we believe, then in Crisis, leaders must create belief that no matter how desperate, how unprecedented the situation may be, we're going to come out on top.

My favorite definition of faith is "the assurance of things hoped for, the conviction of things not seen."[9] This idea of hope and things not seen certainly could be applied to a much more positive set of circumstances like a leader's vision or a personal dream. Yet it feels especially poignant when applied to Crisis. With vision and dreams, there's time. There are steps to take and milestones we can set to mark our progress. In Crisis, the time is now. Milestones? How about this may end *muy pronto*? Crisis brings such acute impact, we often can't begin to think our way out of it in terms of process. It's like being underwater and looking for the lighter colored water to know which way to swim, wishing with everything we have that we're already safely at the surface.

The problem with this is that while Crisis can emerge (or seem to emerge) out of nowhere, its end generally doesn't come about as abruptly. So a measure of endurance is required. And that's where the belief comes in. We're getting our tails bombed for fifty-six days straight, and we're supposed to believe what? On day fourteen, or twenty-eight, or fifty, it's the thing hoped for and not seen. But still, can we believe that in the end—*believing first there will be an end*—when it comes, we will prevail?

FOR REFLECTION

1. What is your level of credibility with your people, such that you are ready to lead and have them respond should you find yourselves in Crisis? What investments should you be making in this? Is your lighthouse operational?

2. What type of readiness and contingency plans do you have in place? What is needed? What forms of Crisis should you anticipate? Are you prepared to carry out your plans?

CHAPTER 5

READINESS

I love movies, always have. I remember as a child seeing a black-and-white *King Kong* at the drive-in theater. I saw the first *Star Wars* release *(Episode IV: A New Hope)* in the theater in 1977. Certain movies effectively define a given generation. For me, *Top Gun* was one such film. I was sixteen when it released, and it was such a cool movie. So, when it was announced that *Top Gun: Maverick* would release in the spring of 2020, I was among those fans who were really pumped. And then came COVID-19, and I had to wait another two years before I could find out what Pete Mitchell had been up to all this time.

One of my favorite scenes from the sequel was the exchange between Maverick and Admiral Beau Simpson, call sign Cyclone, played by Jon Hamm. Maverick's friend and guardian angel Iceman had just died. Cyclone is relieving Maverick of his training duties.

"Sir," Maverick insists, "they're not ready."
Cyclone retorts, "Well, it was your job to get them ready."
"Sir, they have to believe that this mission can be flown."
After Cyclone permanently grounds Maverick, "That is all."

Leading up to this at the onset of training, one brash pilot,

Hangman, had accurately asserted, "We're going into combat on a level that no living pilot has ever seen . . . not even him."

When the mission was moved up a week, Coyote objected, "Sir, no one here has successfully flown the low-level course."

Now, with Maverick out of the picture, a mission that had not ever been done (or even tried), simulated training that had not been successfully completed, was about to take yet another turn. Just not the turn Cyclone intended.

In the transition scene, on her doorstep, Maverick's flame Penny challenges him, "Those are your pilots. If anything happens to them, you'll never forgive yourself."

The next morning, during the flight briefing where Cyclone begins to change the flight parameters, a signal appears on the course. When the tower discovers that it's Maverick entering the course despite no approved flight plan, Maverick simply replies, "I'm going anyway."

"Nice," whispers Phoenix.

With an even more aggressive time target for the run, another pilot, Payback, is incredulous. "2:15? That's impossible."

"Maverick's inbound."[1]

The Model Applied to Readiness

It's been said that you can't fix stupid. That might be true. But an angle we can take here is not about stupidity, but of ignorance. I'm a believer that ignorance is not a damning or even predictive state. It simply means that one hasn't been shown yet. I know virtually nothing about how to maintain an automobile, other than where to take it and at what frequency. Still, I'm confident that it's more about my lack of having been shown than an inability to comprehend or complete a task.

In her TED Talk on growth mindset, Stanford researcher Carol Dweck relayed a story of a teacher that, rather than giving failing grades, gives the grade of "not yet."[2] Ignorance is about that *not yet*, and as leaders in this season, we should also be about that *not yet*.

The *not yet* of a circumstance could very well be a function of experience, or it could be that it really is unprecedented. Either way, as leaders we have an active role to play. And when we think about it, this is a season in which we may have a lot more control. As we equip our people, the *not yet* becomes a "been there, done that," and the season transitions to the next.

What Characterizes Readiness

As we've established, the primary driver in this season is that the challenge is greater than our readiness to take it on. It's natural then that there could be very real doubts. Those doubts may produce any number of derivative emotions: fear, anxiety, intimidation, hopelessness. None of these works for us or our people, which is why belief is so critical to establish.

However, like me, you may have had experience when, rather than doubt, such a scenario produces energy, anticipation, thrill, and excitement. Here, a leader's challenge might include that while this can be done, it's no slam dunk.

Either way, there's much to be discovered, processed, prepared for, put in motion, monitored, and seen through to completion.

Focus/Activity in Readiness

Because the dilemma is about Readiness, this brings in two dimensions to which we've alluded. One is skill. *Do I know how?* The other is motivation. *Do I want to?*

In the introduction, I referred to Situational Leadership. Here, I want to go back to it with more depth as it is a terrific model that deals with the Readiness of a team member, his or her skill and motivation, and the most appropriate approach a leader should take given this.

The magic here is that the leader is taking an informed and *situational* approach to face what's ahead. Whenever I use this in

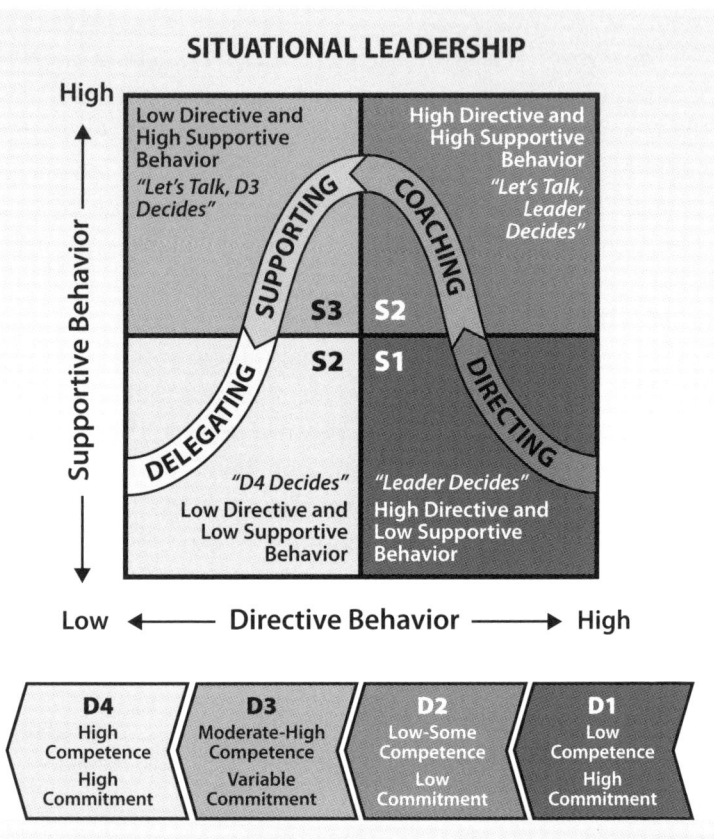

coaching executives or workshops, I like to point out two things in terms of the mindfulness of the leader in their selection on which approach to adopt.

1. **Same task, different person.** What might be routine for one might be completely new to another. For the first, the leader might select a Delegating approach because the team doesn't need a lot of support or direction. For the latter, it might require any of

the other three. Same task, different person. Let's assume the motivation is high and it's just situational ignorance. The leader would take on a much more Directing approach, answering with "Here's how . . ."

2. **Same person, different task.** Odds are, the people on our teams are good at something or they wouldn't be on the team. And, we all have things we enjoy, so motivation isn't a problem. The net result is that in some tasks, team members will have earned that S4, Delegating, approach. But for that task that's not a lot of fun which we tend to avoid or not put our best effort into, S3 Supporting might be in order. Note that the "support" might come with a swift kick in the pants (figuratively, of course) or a stroke of the ego. Again, that depends on the person. But if motivation is high and I just need to be shown, S1 Directing should be in play. Same person, different task.

In our *Top Gun: Maverick* case study, I would argue that S3 Supporting was the choice, and the right one. There was Moderate-High Competence in the pilots. After all, they were the best of the best. Still, none had been asked to do what they were being asked to do *yet*. And, the commitment was somewhat variable. There were looks that conveyed, "Are you serious?" There were degrees of animosity between pilots as well as between at least one of the pilots and Maverick as the instructor. Maverick wisely chose a Supporting style, giving encouragement and building a team. But he also had to be low Directive. He was not in the pilot seat of their plane. Throughout the training, he had to create scenarios to cause the pilots to decide and act on their own, thereby learning from their own experience and ultimately building the belief that they could be successful.

The Leader's Role in Readiness

The primary roles the leader may take in the Readiness season are that of teacher and/or advocate.

After some time in the CEO seat of our leadership center, I vividly remember a time when we were missing on elements of execution across our client projects at a rate that was too high, at least for me. These were primarily small details, mostly unnoticed by the clients, but it was the proverbial "duck on the water" where things may have been looking smooth on the surface but below we were pedaling way, way too hard. It was creating loss in the forms of noise, inefficiency, time, and cost of delivery.

Part of our organizational model was that we had six to eight young staff members on our team who were part of a two-year fellowship program in which we scholarshipped them for their MBAs while they worked for us as full-time project coordinators as their first professional job after college. These were strikingly talented young people, with typically strong motivation. Most of their difficulties came from inexperience.

Taking it a step further, a good measure of our difficulties were stemming from a lack of understanding of the interdependencies of the work. A project coordinator may know their step in the process, but what about the steps that preceded it or were to follow that would be someone else's responsibility? So part of the trick became zooming out of role-specific myopia.

I was one of the more tenured members of our staff and had a pretty good handle "soup to nuts" on what an excellent client experience should be. Frustrated, I was asking aloud why this disconnect was happening when one of the members of my leadership team told me, "Chuck, you have to become a teacher of the business."

Huh?

What she convinced me of is that things I saw as routine, for the most part, were not well understood by these early career pros. So, I went to work. As a very structured, process-driven once-engineer, I began to map out the client project life cycle. I was so adamant about what I was writing, the header above the steps was "We will . . ."

Somewhere down the list, it hit me. Maybe it was a stroke of genius or more likely divine intervention. Whatever it was, I recognized that while accurate, it would be insufficient to simply dictate a list of "we wills." If there was to be lasting effect with the desired outcome, there had to be more. "Why will we?" I recognized I had to answer the question for the rationale behind each step in the process. So, I inserted a column to the left and labeled it "Because our customers . . ." In my mind, every step in the process had to map to client value. Otherwise, why do it?

Because our customers . . .	We will . . .
1.	1.
2.	2.
3.	3.

Here's an overly simple but very real example.

Me: "Are we all set with Customer X?"
Employee: "I haven't heard back from them."
Me: "When's the last time you reached out?"
Employee: "I emailed them about a week ago."
Me: "How many emails do you think they get a day? What if your email was caught in a spam folder? What if their assistant screens their emails and doesn't recognize yours?"
(Silence.)

I recognize the simplicity of this, but it was a very real conversation and it illustrates the point.

Because our customers . . .	We will . . .
1. Are busy running their business 2. Are inundated with emails 3. Have firewalls to protect against emails with attachments that may contain viruses	1. Follow up every email requiring a response with a call letting them know it's been sent and to look for it, leaving a voice mail or message with their assistant if needed. 2. Follow up with another call if necessary within three to four days (or other situationally appropriate window).

Another teaching tactic I would employ is the ride-along. I may be having a meeting with a senior leader of one of our clients. I set the stage with a project coordinator: "You're coming, and you're responsible for taking notes and generating the follow-up document (either back to the client or to our team). We'll review it together before you send it."

Here, they had to own the next steps. Could they pick up on what's important and play it back accurately and concisely? If they missed anything, the review we had would serve as the stopgap as well as tee up the teachable moment for me to say, "Did you catch when she said . . .? Here's why that matters to her and what we need to be thinking . . ." If they were in a Boeing F/A-18F Super Hornet, their hand would be on the joystick. It was the flight debrief that became the second part of the learning lab.

The late Pat Summitt is without question one of the greatest coaches of all time, men's or women's, professional or amateur sports. I have an enduring memory of a documentary where she was described as someone who could have her back turned to the game going on behind her while she was having a teachable moment with players on the bench. She was best-in-class about not missing those.

Leader as Teacher is a real role. So is Leader as Advocate.

Going back to the big screen, I'm among those who had not heard of Dorothy Vaughan before the movie *Hidden Figures*.[3] As cool as he is, I'm not sure Mav can hold a candle to Dorothy Vaughan.

In her NASA biography, she is remembered as a respected mathematician and NASA's first African American manager.[4] Wikipedia refers to her as a "human computer."[5] She was awarded a Congressional Gold Medal and even has a crater on the moon named after her. In an era of Jim Crow segregation rules, even people with working genius were subject to race- and gender-specific workspace. The cinematic version of her story was set in a room full of white men in short-sleeve shirts, black ties, and pocket protectors. It was, in fact, rocket science. Vaughan was depicted as being an advocate for her brilliant young mathematicians who proved every bit the equals of their white male counterparts. The film depicts her as advocate and encourager. The real-life Vaughan reflected on her time there: "I changed what I could, and what I couldn't, I endured."[6] Vaughan simultaneously made a way for her team and effectively role-modeled an ethic that was (literally) world changing.

In the film, Kevin Costner plays Al Harrison, based on the real-life Robert C. Gilruth, head of the Space Task Group at Langley Research Center and later the first director of what is now the Johnson Space Center in Houston. However, the organizational structure of the Space Task Group was much more complicated and was changing quickly during this time period. For clarity in the movie, the management structure is compressed and the composite character Al Harrison was created.[7] While Costner's character is a function of artistic license, I don't think it too much of a stretch that there had to be someone in that management structure who was an advocate for Vaughan and her team for them to even have the chance to contribute at the level they did.

The transferability of this idea, I think, is very real. In times when Readiness is questioned, there are those who will come up with reasons why someone doesn't have what it takes. Some will be rooted in experience and others in bias. Whatever the case, there comes a time when as leaders we have to advocate and go against the grain, reminding the system and the talent in question that they indeed have what it takes, and give them their shot.

The Tone and Message in Readiness

Limitations are challenges, real or perceived. The tone and message from the leader must be "You got this." When a team member is in over their head or on ground they've never treaded before, they need to be equipped with the confidence that whatever they face can be done—and it can be done by them.

I regularly ask people in my practice about the best leaders they've ever been around. The things I often hear include:

- "They believed in me when no one else did. Not even myself."
- "They stood up for me."
- "They got me what I needed to do the job."
- "They spent time with me."
- "They helped me learn from my mistakes."
- "They gave me opportunities."
- "They showed me what mattered and why."

In my experience, one of the most thrilling things in leadership is giving someone a chance in the deep end of the pool and watching them step up to that challenge. It's often the springboard to much bigger things. And, if I'm completely transparent, I love being proven right.

Belief in Readiness

"They have to believe that this mission can be flown."

In a season when the circumstances demand capacity beyond what a team or team member is prepared for, it is vital that the leader establishes this belief in their minds: "This can be done."

Think about it. Without this belief, why bother? Why give up? Why not passively accept whatever is coming? Or better yet, let it be someone else's problem.

Most of us, in our leadership roles, are not facing literal nuclear threats. Still, more than we'd care for, most of us have faced (and will continue to face) figurative nuclear threats that must be addressed. Or, let's take the stakes down a few notches. Let's say that a circumstance is common to organizational leadership, but it's totally new to the team facing it. Because they don't know what they don't know, the impossibility of a situation may be perceived and not real at all. They just don't know it yet.

Regardless, it's incumbent on the leader to instill a belief in themselves that they can be successful.

FOR REFLECTION

1. What leader was a great teacher or advocate for you? What has that translated into since? How can you pay that forward? With whom?

2. If someone is struggling to perform at an expected standard, what part of that problem do you own? Where could (or should) you become more of a teacher of the business?

3. Are there challenges where you need to demonstrate what's possible to mentees who may not have the confidence or belief that something can be done?

4. Where's the line between letting someone struggle—or even fail—in the learning experience and showing them how to do it? How do you determine where that line is?

CHAPTER 6

PEAK

At age twenty, Sir Andrew Lloyd Webber collaborated with Tim Rice on a fifteen-minute pop contata to be performed by a prep school choir. That composition was the genesis of the musical *Joseph and the Amazing Technicolor Dreamcoat*, which went on to thousands of performances over seven decades.[1]

The project stuck remarkably close to the Genesis 37–50 account of the baby brother-turned-senior adviser to the pharoah, with Webber taking literary license primarily with the playful entertainment value for the audience. The climax of the story is the ultimate reunification of Joseph's family through a series of events sparked by a famine. This famine lasted seven years and had followed seven years of prosperity. This sequence had been foretold through Joseph's interpretation of the pharoah's troubling dreams.

In Webber's version, the pharoah bore a striking resemblance to Elvis, a king who had it all and was clearly on top of his game. It was a season of Peak, and Joseph proved just the man to lead through the seven years of prosperity in preparation for the season that would follow.

The Wind at Your Back

Over the last ten years, I've gotten into road cycling. To be clear, I'm not more than a weekend warrior. To do cycling at a high level requires time in the saddle that I simple don't have, not to mention a gene pool that I also don't have.

About the time I got into the sport, I had lunch at our local Mexican restaurant (training food, no doubt) with Steve, a fellow cyclist who was much more experienced than I. Our leadership center was just getting into creating more original digital content, and we were looking at doing a project using cycling as a metaphor for high-performance teams. I was picking Steve's brain about the relevant aspects of cycling to help set up our storyboard.

In that conversation, one of the things that came up was the descent on a particular route near our town. That descent, along with the prevailing wind that was often at your back, afforded an opportunity to go *really* fast. These are not speeds of professional riders, but for a bunch of amateurs (at least *this* amateur), exceeding forty miles per hour on a bicycle with twenty-three-millimeter-width tires is pretty doggone fast—and not my favorite thing.

I recall Steve's animated expression at the thrill he derived from these opportunities when he said, between dips in the bowl of salsa, "There are only so many chances you get to go forty-five miles per hour!" Uh, yeah . . .

The Model Applied to Peak

In Peak, all the conditions are favorable, or at least those that count the most: market forces, competitive advantage in your product or service, the right people in the right seats, etc. Heck, in times of Peak with macroeconomic factors, even poorly run organizations can do well. Success may vary in degree, but it's still success—and it can be terribly misleading.

When I joined Soderquist Leadership in 2005, things were really good, or so it seemed. Yet, for so many other businesses it proved in time to be a season of overinvestment, risky bets, and unsustainable "growth" that led into the Great Recession of 2008 to 2009. Those seemingly favorable conditions were masking underperformance. Companies may have been up 10 percent year-over-year, but their market segment may have been up 20 percent. Or while a company was up 20 percent, if they had they actually done what they were capable of, perhaps they could have reached 30 percent, leaving too much opportunity on the table.

A similar dynamic happened at the onset of the pandemic. I was leading CEO peer advisory groups at that time made up of high-performing leaders in high-performing companies. While everyone was affected by COVID-19, some firms actually outperformed their pre-pandemic performance. Conditions had shifted where they could capture new ground (and go *really* fast) when the larger narrative was that the world had literally turned upside down. These examples included a jeweler whose sales spiked, causing stressors in stocking enough inventory and replenishment. A company that did construction of outdoor living spaces for homeowners, particularly wealthy homeowners, found itself in Peak. For both businesses, people with disposable income who couldn't travel redirected those dollars other ways.

Another member with expertise in procurement and supply chain was able to expand their business in securing and distributing needed supplies like KN95 masks (note: this was not a case of profiteering) while another medical company was able to develop their own approved rapid COVID-19 test to help with demand where supply simply could not keep up to support the health-care needs of the region.

The lesson here is that Peak can come in the most unexpected circumstances, but it's still Peak.

It would be reasonable to think that leading in Peak would be easy. Yet as one CEO shared with me, it's not about leadership being relatively easier or harder as seasons vary. In that context, leadership is more of a constant—it just has different input that demands different output. Still, it should not be taken for granted, and if an organization is to take full advantage of this special time, leaders have to recognize it and lead in ways that capture the full force of the momentum working in their favor.

What Characterizes Peak

When a company is at Peak, people can feel it. Perhaps it is because it's such a contrast to all of the other seasons that have some form of dilemma to address. Actually, it's not the absence of dilemmas; they just take different forms. Let's look at two.

Keeping up. In Peak, it can seem that opportunities are presenting themselves at every turn. The diligent opportunist can't begin to think of bypassing a deal that will drive growth. So, she doubles down, typically with good reason. New business bringing new volume is great, particularly if it can be done without expanding your footprint of fixed costs. It might also drive margins such that it provides an opportunity to reinvest in the business to either address lingering issues in infrastructure or build new platforms to sustain the growth.

One risk Peak brings in this approach is stressing people and systems in trying to keep up. If the answer is people who are not able to take time off, machines that are having their scheduled preventative maintenance bypassed, staff working longer hours, or sustaining higher velocity while maintaining quality of work, at some point the company is risking breakdown.

The rationale of responding to opportunities in this way is natural. After all, a leader knows that if their company does not step up to meet demand, someone else will, and they may not get another crack at the new business anytime soon. They also know that their stakeholders—ownership, board, and investors— expect them to drive those positive results. Bypassing opportunity can be unthinkable, if not unforgivable. Keeping up follows the old saying, "Get while the gettin's good."

Even in the stress of keeping up, this is typically viewed as a positive. Let's face it—people like to win. It's a heckuva lot better than losing. Putting points up on the board is fun. It brings energy. Bells are ringing and high fives are slapping all around. It can be a rush, particularly in the moment, even if people, processes, and equipment are being pushed to their limit.

Complacency. On the other end of the spectrum is complacency. This probably requires little explanation, but when conditions are favorable and it doesn't take a lot of effort to gain new business and post results, the risk of letdown is real. For some, the rationale can be "Why put in the effort if I can get the results I'm used to with less?" Let's face it, if winning is fun, winning with little effort can be really fun.

The problem here is obvious. When things turn (and they will), it's difficult to simply flip the switch on effort and have results turn back on in turn. Someone may have just come along and moved your cheese.[2]

Ultimately, Peak is most notably characterized by opportunity, growth, fun, speed, positivity, energy, and celebration—however we decide to react to it.

Focus/Activity in Peak

By and large, Peak presents conditions in which most leaders want to capture the opportunities. As such, productivity becomes the name of the game. In manufacturing, productivity looks like assets running at full capacity, and volume per unit time is the Key Performance Indicator. In sales, productivity looks like new customers and growing new business with existing customers.

This focus on productivity drives activity of people to maximize volume. Processes are tweaked to maximize execution. New people are brought in, even if it's contract or temporary help. Purchasing new equipment is far easier to justify if the volume is there. The prevailing question is "What *else* can we do?"

Another area of focus is the market on a number of dimensions. The first to consider is the immediate conditions.

How are your customers doing? Are their actions or attitudes changing at all? This is true B2C or B2B.

Another dimension is the supporting infrastructure necessary to run the business. For example, can your supply chain keep up? Can your distribution network serve the volume you are likely to produce? Do you have access to capital to fund accelerated activity?

A third market dimension is macroeconomic factors. To me, there are a few almost universal indicators. Two are energy and transportation. Energy, whether it's oil and gas or alternative energy, affects all of us every day. Transportation is less obvious, but I once heard an economist quip that every time something is produced or purchased, something is shipped. What's happening with inflation, interest rates, consumer confidence, legislative activity, and geopolitical dynamics can all play a role as well.

The key in focusing on macroeconomic factors is to understand which factors are likely influencing your ability to produce, your customers' ability to buy, and your suppliers' ability to, well, supply. It's also an exercise in understanding how long it's likely to last. This leads us to an activity in prudence—contingency planning. (Think back to the story of Joseph and Pharoah.) At its core, contingency planning is about identifying what can change that could impact your performance, monitoring it closely, recognizing potential triggers that would merit taking action, and knowing how to respond when the trigger is flipped.

The Leader's Role in Peak

The leader's role is pretty clear at Peak. With a productivity focus, the leader becomes a driver. This blend makes sure every part of the business is hitting on all cylinders, providing necessary resources, knocking down barriers, and maybe even leading the band.

Simultaneously, as the driver, the leader declares war on

complacency, not being satisfied, knowing the risk that backing off can bring. Some leaders may interpret this as cracking the whip, not something I'd advocate. A healthier expression of the motivation would be the leader mounting a horse and shouting "Charge!" Recall back in chapter 2, we looked at the SWOT matrix[3] and the intersection of strength and opportunity. This quadrant was labeled Invest. Same idea.

To further illustrate, in my time at Soderquist Leadership, often we would encounter an objection on a given project centered on culture, leadership or team development, strategy, or the like with the rationale that "It's just not the right time. Maybe when things pick back up." The problem with this thinking is that when things are good, it may just be the worst time to pull resources from the business in favor of development.

If we were to look again at competitive cycling, it's the competitors whose strength is the descent that try to attack the field, knowing they have the advantage and a unique moment to gain time against the field. Coasting is the last thing on their mind; instead, it's crouch even lower for better aerodynamics and pedal even harder.

The Tone and Message in Peak

The tone and message from the leader should ultimately convey a sense of urgency:

- Time is money.
- Opportunities missed are opportunities lost forever.
- We can capture new ground.
- We can gain advantage over our competitors.
- It is time!

It's this sense of urgency that, if permeating through the organization, has everyone on their A game.

Belief in Peak

The primary belief a leader needs people to adopt is "This is great, *and* it won't last." It's the power of the "and" that matters here. The "great" part stems from the momentum everyone is feeling. That part isn't that hard. The "it won't last" component is what brings the sense of urgency, the antidote for complacency.

Recall our transplanted hero in Egypt after his capture in the book of Genesis. Not only did Joseph make sure productivity was high, he planned for the turn—seven years of famine that would follow. He did not allow wasted opportunity. Instead, he put food in storage that would be necessary to sustain them through the famine. The biblical account compared the volume to "the sand of the sea, until he ceased to measure it, for it could not be measured."[4] This foresight, planning, and execution positioned Egypt not only to take care of its own people, but the Bible states that "moreover, all the earth came to Egypt to Joseph to buy grain, because the famine was severe over all the earth."[5]

Here, Joseph knew the prosperity wouldn't last. Clearly, one could argue that his positional authority was enough to cause so much grain to be stored. Joseph was not going to be able to do that on his own. When the boss says so, compliant workers will do as they are told (particularly in ancient Egypt). Still, we might be able to imagine how much incremental productivity was gained because people, including Pharoah himself, believed what Joseph needed them to believe.

A Final Case[6]

I've been counted among Chick-fil-A's raving fans for years. They have proven to crack the code for excellence in quick-serve restaurants. They are a standard by which others are measured and a reference point for other industries on how to operate. They are studied and written about as continuously as the lines in their drive-through lanes.

In 2009, I had the distinct privilege of hosting Chick-fil-A's executive committee at the retreat center in Northwest Arkansas operated by Soderquist Leadership. Three years earlier, a mutual friend had introduced me to the Cathy brothers, Dan and Bubba. I was set to accompany our founding executive, Don Soderquist, to Atlanta for a speaking engagement. Don had retired from Walmart Stores in 2003 as senior vice chairman. After a few calls back and forth, the details were ironed out that led to the formation of a great friendship between Don and the Chick-fil-A executive committee.

That group knew well Don's role in Walmart's growth after Sam Walton's death, partnering with Sam's successor as CEO, David Glass. Not only did the company continue to grow, it's culture was nurtured and protected such that it was not lost. Many would argue it was strengthened. This doesn't happen on its own. Don was known as "Keeper of the Culture" after Mr. Sam's death. And Don would be the first to tell anyone he did not do it on his own either. But growth with culture was not a mistake. Rather, it was the product of intense attention the company's leadership gave it.

This trip to Northwest Arkansas had the sole purpose of talking to Don, trying to understand the Walmart experience and what they could learn. This executive team was made up of Dan Cathy, Bubba Cathy, Steve Robinson, Buck McCabe, Perry Ragsdale, and Tim Tassopoulos. They were on a yearlong quest, visiting four established experts in various fields, one each quarter, to see what they could learn and reapply to strengthen the company.

We should be clear that they were at Peak and understood that while things were going great, they were not immune to struggle. They acknowledged that while this group had been together for over twenty years through their careers in the company, this would be the last decade this team would be together. They understood their responsibility to position the company for a series of successions and a future that did not include them. At their annual operators meeting a year earlier, Jim Collins had told the audience that if the company ceased to exist, there would be "an unfillable hole." Apparently they got the message.

For two days, this group met with the retired retail icon, picking his brain on every topic imaginable. I was just a young executive who was graciously allowed to be a fly on the wall. So many things about that trip left an impression on me, but what was shouting was how keenly aware they were that Peak would not last on its own.

Later, this group did an open roundtable debrief of these experiences at the new year's annual operator meeting. In that conversation, it was Robinson who reminded the group that it was back in 1982 when we "got ourselves into a little bit of trouble." That experience and what they did to course correct were clearly etched in this group's mind. Robinson wondered how the company would retain a sense of "productive paranoia" that Collins challenged them with.

This leadership team understood its past, its present state, and enough about its future that it did the hard work, made it transparent for everyone to see, and along the way got people to believe what it believed.

Over the next ten years, one executive after another retired and a successor took over his responsibilities. In 2021, Dan Cathy's eldest son, Andrew, became the company's third CEO, following his father and grandfather. When Dan became president in 2001, the company's sales had just topped $1 billion. By 2020, that number had grown to $14.1 billion with 2,627 restaurants,[7] and there is no sign of the company sloughing off anytime soon.

FOR REFLECTION

1. Where does your organization fall on the continuum between keeping up and complacency? Where might you be overstressing your people and processes? Where might you be getting a little too comfortable and lazy?

2. How are you keeping score such that it's not just about volume and busyness, but rather about optimizing your mix and maximizing profitability? How do you know you are not losing by doing more?

3. What do you need to be doing now to prepare for when the season changes to less favorable conditions? Think contingency or scenario planning, building up reserves, and developing people in ways that best happen in these conditions.

CHAPTER 7

TROUGH

The circular flow model in economics presents a theory of how money flows through society.[1] While it's a bit more complicated than this, in its simplest form, money flows from those who sell resources to firms that produce goods and services that are sold to the public. Meanwhile, those same firms pay wages to their employees, which allows them to spend on others' goods and

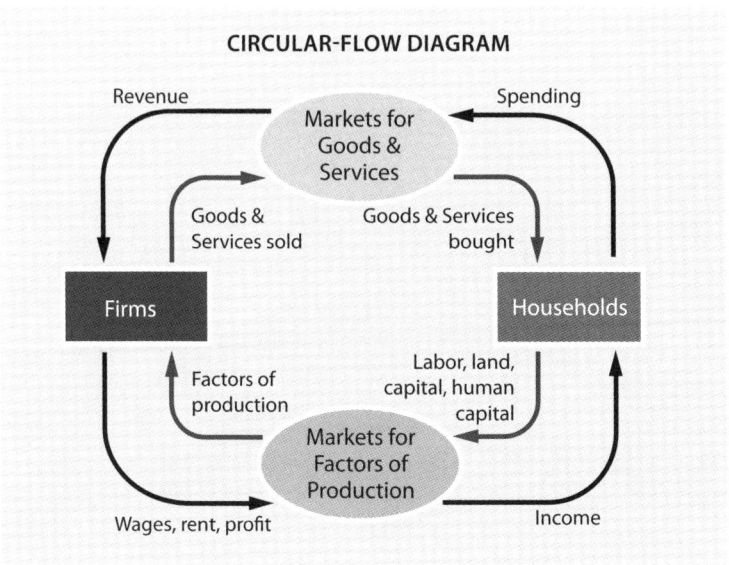

services. It's an endless cycle of money.

I have a friend who has lived in the inner city of Chicago for over thirty years, in the neighborhood of North Lawndale. Just blocks from his home is another neighborhood, Little Village. Little Village is primarily made up of immigrants from Mexico. It's a remarkable section of society in many ways, including in its commercial enterprise.

On one of my trips to see my friend, he shared that a dollar will change hands in Little Village nineteen times before it leaves the neighborhood. Think about that in light of the circular flow model. The bakery employs a person who spends money at the sporting goods store, whose owner and employees spend money at the clothing store, whose employees spend at the jewelry store, and so on. Throughout the neighborhood, goods and services are being purchased and sold: rent and mortgages are being paid, groceries are bought, haircuts given, and on and on it goes.

This microeconomy is so dynamic. This two-mile stretch on Twenty-Sixth Street, graced by a decorative arch on one end and a Sam's Club on the other, does more business in a day than

many other streets in Chicago, including the Magnificent Mile of Michigan Avenue with storefronts like Tiffany & Co., Nike, Gucci, and Tommy Bahama.[2]

I cannot claim to be an economist, and politics aside, this model makes a lot of sense to me. When cash is flowing (and not just credit), it produces an interrelated vibrancy where all boats are being lifted. But what happens when the velocity of the flow slows? What happens when someone in the system decides not to spend? Or supply chain factors, labor, or interest rates force a slowdown in the spending or redirecting of funds out of the system to creditors or the government?

When this happens for an extended period, the ripple effect through this ecosystem is ultimately felt by all, and we find ourselves in a Trough. For the purpose of our seasonal leadership model, Trough is the inverted curve of Peak. The wind is not at our back; it's squarely in our face.

When we think of Trough, it's natural that we would think of macroeconomic factors. The Great Recession of 2008 to 2009 had widespread impacts brought on by the housing market and mortgage lending crisis. The terrorist attacks of September 11, 2001, brought a slowdown in many markets. At the time of this writing, headwinds include rising interest rates, a shrinking labor pool, rising wages, and challenging supply chain issues in many markets. This was preceded by the economic impact of the COVID-19 pandemic when seemingly everything shut down. In the United States, multiple stimulus packages were installed to try to jump-start the circular flow.

Still, it's important to recognize that Trough can exist on a much smaller scale, even within a single enterprise. This could come from the loss of key team members; of competitive advantage; of a key supplier, distributor, or other partner; of access to capital, and the like. Everything and everyone around you may be doing fine, but you're in a daily struggle just to make it.

The Model Applied to Trough

Whenever I'm asked to speak to a group of emerging leaders, students, or a high-capacity, early-career audience, one of the themes I tend to hit on is "So you want to be a leader." The reason I spend time on this is that too often, a less informed, less experienced view of leadership is limited to perks we associate with it: title, pay, the office, the car, etc. (In one of my stops at Kimberly-Clark, there was actually talk of how many ceiling panels were in each office. Were you in a four-panel office? Six? Eight? Twenty-four? There was a direct correlation to the number of panels and where one sat on the food chain—or org chart, as it were.)

As real as those things can be, the problem is that view of leadership underestimates, if not omits altogether, the concept of Trough, and what's just as real about it as is real with perks.

What Characterizes Trough

In this period of inversion, resulting emotions and morale are all down for a sustained period. There's not a lot of fun to be had. In fact, if fun begins to emerge at any level, even for a good reason, it can somehow feel misplaced.

People ask:

- "How long will this last?"
- "What's being done about this?"
- "How did we get here in the first place?"
- "Who's to blame?"
- "Do I need to jump ship?"

Volume is down. Things feel quiet and slow, because they are. Attempts at course correction produce little, if any, material or lasting results. Uncertainty gives rise to doubt. Anxiety and weariness can follow.

Focus/Activity in Trough

Because of the inherent negativity of a prolonged Trough, it's easy for the collective mindset to major on what isn't or can't be done because of it. This is a function of the natural downward spiral an organization can experience. It follows that a leader needs to disrupt that momentum by shifting the focus to what *can* be done. Remember the Serenity Prayer:

> God, grant me the serenity to accept the things
>   I cannot change,
> the courage to change the things I can,
> and the wisdom to know the difference.[3]

To this, the organization must look to where it can find and create value. Resourcefulness, when resources are hard to come by, is a key ingredient.

In my first stop at Kimberly-Clark, one of the euphemisms that would come up in these times was "painting lines." It did, in fact, involve painting lines, but it was the symbol for all things deferred maintenance. Consider that the facility was a few hundred thousand square feet of manufacturing and warehouse space; there were a lot of yellow caution lines used to demark traffic flow for pedestrians and forklifts or other vehicular traffic. Lines also existed to demark rows for material storage. In time, these lines would wear down, so if there was a period where volume was down and it made no sense to build inventory by producing more or to have idle labor, machine crews would grab a brush and a can of yellow paint and paint some lines.

In no way would this have been anyone's first choice. No one was making any money in the circular flow model unless you were selling paint or paint brushes, yet it still made sense to turn activity to things that needed attention, that were important to the workplace (i.e., added value), and that had been left unattended for any number of reasons. Trough can create the opportunity to catch up on things that actually make the business healthier.

Trough also presents an opportunity for some real introspection. Trough periods can come about by external forces where we have no control or influence. But the hard reality is that Troughs can also be brought about by things we have done or have left undone. Leaders have to be the role models for accepting responsibility for this and for stating that the status quo is unacceptable. Too often, if we're not careful, we get busy addressing symptoms and not the root of the problem.

One of my favorite takeaways from my time at K-C was our commitment to Kepner-Tregoe Problem Solving and Decision Making tools.[4] Undoubtedly, my affinity for the model is that I'm a nerd and I like structure, but the legitimate reason is that it prompts a deeper analysis of what's going on—yes, recognizing symptoms but by truly identifying root cause. It starts with the identification of a problem statement. That may sound obvious, but a well-crafted problem statement is the launch point for what's really going on and what we might be able to do about it. We ask, "Where and when is the problem happening? Where and when is it not happening?" We explore all possible causes in order to identify the most likely causes and ultimately the root cause.

When we can get to the root, our odds of meaningful and sustained course correction are infinitely better than a symptom-based approach, or simply sitting around waiting for the wind to change.

The Leader's Role in Trough

There are at least two roles the leader has in periods of Trough: promoting and multiplying encouragement and resolve. The encouragement is simply a recognition that things are, indeed, tough. To try to mask reality is futile and risks a loss of credibility for the leader because they may be seen as phony or out of touch—or *both*. It's a great spot for empathy. After all, the hardship is shared. It's also a great spot for sympathy—recognizing that the shared experience may be having unique impacts on any given team member. Here, the leader can communicate that they care and, in doing so, ascribe value to each person.

Leading and producing resolve in the organization has a harder, more firm feel but is equally as appropriate. It is tenacity, determination, an act of will that produces a spirit that we will keep on keeping on through whatever difficulties we are experiencing. It's the unwillingness to give up or give in. It's what allows leaders to continue trying after prior attempts to produce change have failed. It's the ability to make hard decisions. It's the commitment to communication that gives everyone involved visibility to what's being done and why, what we know today, and what we're looking for tomorrow.

The Tone and Message in Trough

Once again, the tone and message in Trough are all about endurance. If we want people to believe that they can endure, then it's the central theme through prolonged difficulty. One of the most poignant examples of this comes from Vice Admiral James Stockdale.

A statue of Stockdale stands outside the school of leadership at the United States Naval Academy in Annapolis, Maryland. One of the panels on the statue reads:

> Vice Admiral James Bond Stockdale was one of the most highly decorated officers in the history of the United States Navy and the only three-star admiral to wear both aviator wings and the Medal of Honor. As a result of his heroic actions, he was awarded 26 combat decorations including two Distinguished Flying Crosses, three Distinguished

Service Medals, four Silver Star Medals, and two Purple Hearts.[5]

A second panel reads:

As senior prisoner of war in Vietnam from 1965 to 1973, Vice Admiral James Stockdale's dynamic leadership and extreme heroism saved hundreds of American lives and permitted them to return home with honor. Despite the enemy's unrelenting attempts to break his will, his eternal defiance and valor in the face of unthinkable odds will forever serve as an inspiration to all Americans in uniform.

Years after Stockdale's release as a POW and his return to the United States, author and Stanford University researcher Jim Collins asked him what made the difference for the prisoners who survived the POW camp and those who did not. According to Stockdale, some of those who died as prisoners gave up quickly, without the motivation to endure, seeing no hope for their release. On the other end of the spectrum, a second subgroup also did not survive. This group tended to be overly optimistic of their pending release and would set arbitrary dates as predicted timing for their freedom. "We'll be out by Easter . . . by Christmas . . ." Easters and Christmases would come and go, and this group would effectively die of a broken heart.

In sharp contrast, according to Stockdale, those who survived had an entirely different view. Based on what Stockdale said,

Collins coined what became known as the Stockdale Paradox:

> You must maintain unwavering faith that you can and will prevail in the end, regardless of the difficulties, and at the same time, have the discipline to confront the most brutal facts of your current reality, whatever they might be.[6]

Some subscribe to the approach of "fake it till you make it." I do not. In Trough, it can be tempting to take this position, rationalizing that as leaders, we must put on a good show that things are actually OK so people will feel better and not be unnecessarily bothered by the accuracy of their circumstance. I would argue that it risks prolonging or worsening the situation by masking reality. It's a relatively low view of people, but it also fails to enroll them in the solution to the shared difficulty.

Most people in leadership roles will never experience the hardship of a POW camp. Still, if we can apply the lesson found in the Stockdale Paradox, we can set a foundation for endurance for our people. Modeling resolve can produce it in them. Calling hard things for what they are builds credibility by being in touch and sharing the hardship others are feeling.

Belief in Trough

In Trough, the main thing a leader needs people to buy in to is endurance. Here, the dynamics are consistent with those of Crisis in chapter 4. The difference is the acute, immediate nature of Crisis contrasted with the prolonged, "How long will this last?" nature of Trough. Our definition of faith ("the assurance of things hoped for, the conviction of things not seen") still holds. It's just being put to a different test of time. And, just as in Crisis and as demonstrated by the Stockdale Paradox, can we believe that there is an end, and can we endure to the time when that end comes?

An extraordinary case study in endurance is told in *Endurance* by Alfred Lansing, which chronicles the trials and fate of Sir Ernest Shackleton and his ship's crew on its voyage to the Antarctic.[7] In fact, the ship was aptly named *Endurance*. The account of what these men endured is beyond imagination. How they ultimately survived in the face of everything going wrong that could go wrong is a testament to this idea of faith, hope, and conviction.

Another exemplar to me is Dr. Martin Luther King Jr. and his leadership in civil rights in the United States. A strong argument can be made that even in the 2020s, many things must still be endured by people of color in our nation. But in the 1960s, at the height of the civil rights movement, one of Dr. King's themes was that of endurance. Without question, he was calling for peaceful change—change that should start happening now with the realization that endurance will be a critical ingredient to change being realized.

In a speech at the National Cathedral in Washington, DC in 1968, King said,

> "We shall overcome because the arc of the moral universe is long but it bends toward justice."[8] It seems that he knew better than anyone that remarkable endurance would be required to realize the change he dreamed of and for which he so strongly advocated.

This theme perhaps can be best summed up by Pete Seeger's well-known song "We Shall Overcome," which became a hymn of the civil rights movement.

FOR REFLECTION

1. Do you have an accurate and complete picture of your organization's circular flow? Who are you dependent on or sourcing from? Who depends on you, and what value are you adding? Even if you, as a leader, see it, do your people?

2. What stories of endurance do you have in your organization's history? What have you learned from those? Are you using those as "reasons to believe" in building confidence in your people?

3. What activities naturally get deferred in your normal course of business? How can you allocate resources to these in Trough periods to stay "full" while catching up on legitimately value-added activity that promotes your shared long-term organizational health?

CHAPTER 8

ACQUISITION

On July 18, 1995, Kimberly-Clark Corporation announced that it had agreed to buy Scott Paper Company for about $7 billion in stock.[1] The deal closed on December 12 of that same year. Of course, this was big news inside the company, but most of us within the rank and file wondered how the acquisition would affect any of us, if at all.

At the time, I had no idea who "Chainsaw" Al Dunlap was or that he would net reportedly $90 to $100 million personally from the deal.[2] The internal scuttle was that the deal would allow us to gain a dominant share of the tissue business in Europe, where we'd had some difficulty in penetrating the market.

OK, sounds smart. We knew the deal brought big brands like Scott, Cottonelle, and Viva. K-C primarily had premium brands while Scott was more known for value brands. We had stuff they didn't have and vice versa. Of course, P&G wasn't too thrilled with the idea and pursued some antitrust objections, ultimately blocking part of the deal, particularly in Scott's wet wipes business where K-C already had a dominant position. Three guesses on who bought it? P&G.[3]

Such was the competitive drama within the consumer packaged goods industry, and I recall a certain feeling of satisfaction, bordering on thrill, that I was part of a company that bought another company. It made a lot of sense, and everyone seemed to be the better for it.

In the months that followed the necessary integration of the two companies, we had internal language that referred to "K-C heritage" (aka, the way we do it and/or our stuff) and "Scott heritage" (aka, the way they do it and their stuff). The language actually had utility in helping literally tens of thousands of people sort through at any given time on any given topic what we were talking about, historic origins of the moving parts, and ultimately what we were going to agree to going forward.

Twenty-seven years later, and I have now been exposed to a lot more talk of mergers and acquisitions than I ever dreamed of, mostly from clients who were considering a sale or looking for a purchase that complemented and strengthened their position. These advantages come in the forms of brand alignment, new markets, shared markets, and operational efficiencies. In the end, it's a "we're better together than we are apart" rationale that pulls that trigger.

One idea I tend to subscribe to is that the term "M & A" is a little bit of a misnomer. While not 100 percent true nor empirically proven, my experience is that it's a lot less "M" than "A" when we talk about mergers and acquisitions. Even when we call something a merger, there tends to be an acquirer and the one acquired. One tends to be the dominant force in what follows. That can be in the branding, decisions about organizational structure and authority, physical space, or any number of practical components in play. As such, this dynamic can certainly come into play as we consider what leadership looks like in the season of Acquisition.

The Model Applied to Acquisition

Among the seasons we're discussing, Acquisition may be the most undeniable and clearly marked. Yesterday, certain things were true. Today, that's a little bit different because some people signed some documents. Perhaps more than any other season, Acquisition has a clear time stamp that indicates a new season has started.

Regardless of how big or small and no matter how seamless we anticipate the acquisition to go, in my experience leaders should recognize the need for organizational clarity, the anticipated impact of synthesis, and our role in helping people process and get their heads around the change. Even if one believes that "we're better together," they next need to understand how to interpret and internalize the implications that make that true, and they're likely going to need some help in getting there.

What Characterizes Acquisition

Because Acquisition by nature brings change, many of the same things we've covered in other seasons apply here: uncertainty leading to anxiety, possible sense of loss of "how things used to be," maybe shock and denial, and if you're on the right side of the acquisition, even high energy, anticipation, and high fives all around. To be sure, beauty may well be in the eye of the beholder when it comes to an acquisition.

Given all those possibilities, a few unique characteristics in an Acquisition season function to bring two separate and distinct things into one.

The first is a question of trust. "Can I trust you?" After all, we just met. Perhaps we were competitors. If there is any level of perceived threat brought on to my status quo by the change, it's likely that we will have to earn each other's trust—and that will take some time, maybe a lot of time depending on the circumstance.

Keep in mind that trust may not be just character-based trust (i.e., Are you ethical, safe, etc.?). It would likely include competency-based trust (i.e., Are you good at your job? Can I count on you to get me what I need? Can I count on you to take what I give you and handle it properly?). Trust comes with reps. When the rep cycle or contact point is high, that could be established pretty readily. However if the rep cycle is less frequent, it will naturally take much longer.

A second chracteristic is competition. "Are we competing?" Possible answers are, "You bet your @#$Q@," "No, of course not," and "It never occurred to me." Where would competition emerge? Part of it could be just establishing a new pecking order. Whatever the case, a new group must be formed, goals aligned, and productive energy applied. In the 1960s, Bruce Tuckman developed his Stages of Group Development: Forming, Storming, Norming, Performing.[4] Both the ideas of trust and sorting through the competition are evident and arguably necessary for the newly formed "group" to experience in the first three phases

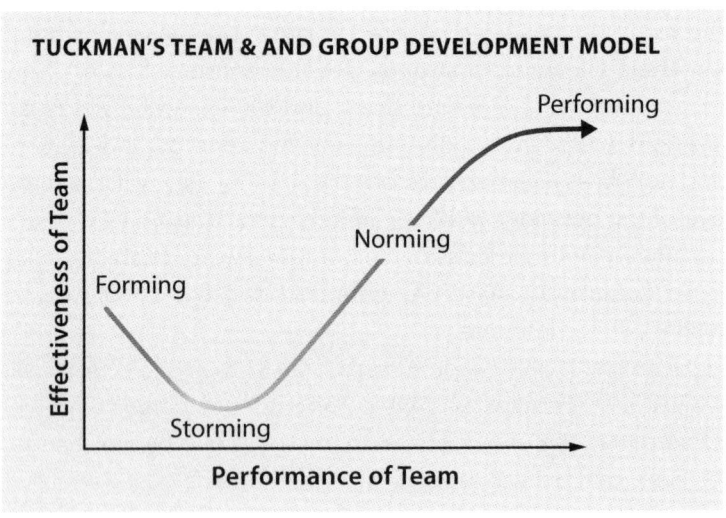

before we can *RE*-establish the Performing portion of the curve.

Among the myriad of possible dynamics of Acquisition and the first three phases of Tuckman's curve, I'll offer two final considerations: resentment and clarity.

Resentment. One may ask, "How could you resent me? You

don't even know me!" It might not matter. One of the things that happens frequently is the consolidation of otherwise redundant functions and capacity. This starts at the highest levels. Two CEOs are generally not a good idea. Do you need two CFOs? Likely not. So the C-suite is for sure affected. Shared services are another area where "efficiencies" are realized: purchasing, IT, accounting, etc. Prior to the merger, each independent organization necessarily had these in place. Post-deal, you really only need one set of most of these functions.

It's less true operationally since volume still needs to be processed (unless you're facing the dilemma of Callahan Auto Parts in *Tommy Boy* when Ray Zalinsky just wanted the brand after Big Tom's untimely death[5]). In all seriousness, this is when things can get deeply personal. If team members of either organization are displaced, that can sting—and not just for those now looking for a new job. Those who remain feel the sting, losing their coworker, friend, mentor. While not the fault of the new guy or new gal, they're the ones within reach when I dish out just how I feel about it all. This can also be true even if everyone was retained but some had to find a new seat on the bus. Through squinted eyes and pursed lips, it can be "Why did they choose *you*?"

Clarity. Not every acquisition comes with resentment, but I'd argue 100 percent of them, without exception, come with a clarity issue. That is, people are seeking it. The search for clarity comes in many forms:

- "Here's how we used to handle this. How did you?"
- "Where do I find the ____?"
- "Who do I talk to in order to ____?"
- "I thought I was supposed to take care of that."
- "I thought you were supposed to take care of that."

Even if things aren't changing in certain areas (even most

areas), people need to know it and are searching for those answers.

Focus/Activity in Acquisition

Several years ago, I had the opportunity to tour the new multimillion-dollar home of a friend of my extended family. I remember one large room in which I was told, "This carpet has no seams." I only know enough about carpet to know what happens when it buckles. I've never laid carpet myself, but I've replaced the carpet in my home once and built a couple of homes in our past. Because of this one-time exposure to truly seamless carpet, carpet seams are now something that just kind of naturally draws my attention.

I've not come across an acquisition where the goal was not seamless, or at least as seamless as possible. Even though much work needs to be done, as much as we can, we want the work, work product, and our customer experience to feel like business as usual.

Internally, the major headings are people and process—what should happen, how it should happen, and by whom. My first job out of school was as a process engineer. In that job, we were always trying to achieve a level of steady state. If a disruption was introduced, our goal was to return to steady state as quickly and cost-effectively as possible. The same is true in Acquisition. To the degree our steady state gets disrupted, we're trying to get things back there. Process seams or even breakdowns can emerge from different methods and tools that are retained and simultaneously employed. (Think software systems as an example.) But if these processes change because one gives way to another or both go away for a completely new process, it can take some time before familiarity and mastery are reacquired to allow the new organization to function at pre-acquisition levels of performance.

When it comes to people, we've already talked about

clarity. There may also be a season of acquiring new skills or new understanding of processes and tools. Maybe it's about training and new skills. It's also about the emotional components that we've identified here. New groups may figure out Tuckman's phases on their own, but it should not be assumed or taken for granted. Instead, leaders should proactively facilitate (literally, "make easy") getting people what they need in order to function at their best. The quicker we can onboard our people to the new reality, the quicker we get back to steady state, or to an *even higher* steady state than what was possible before.

Externally, we have to pay attention to customers, stakeholders, investors, donors, and literally anyone with a stake in the new organization. They're looking for confidence that their interests, at worst, are not adversely affected. If they improve, well all the better. On closer examination, I think we can center back on processes and people. Have key contacts changed between organizations? Have coworking processes been affected in any way?

As with our carpet metaphor, the more seamless we can make this both feel and literally be, the more we can channel our energy and efforts to our work and less so to the seams that could otherwise trip us up.

The Leader's Role in Acquisition

In order for a newly formed organization to truly become unified, the neutral, shared concept needs to be integration. As such, the leader's role, if we're to accelerate through change, trust issues, clarity, and a new orientation so that we're aligned, is that of a bridge builder.

Bridges effectively connect sides where interests, goals, ways of working, and identity were specific and unique. Rare is the occasion when an acquisition simply folds an organization into a holding company design and everything else is left alone. Most of the time, we're looking to gain advantage. Whether the bridge is a connector so that people, resources, and information flow where before it couldn't—or if the bridge is the mechanism where one side is abandoned and the people, resources, and information must cross over to a new space, it's the leader who becomes the chief bridge builder.

To illustrate this, I want to share the basics of story of a nonprofit organization in Northwest Arkansas (NWA). While your acquisition may have more or less scale or complexity, I would argue this case study illustrates well the fundamentals of what's at stake in a season of Acquisition.

The Single Parent Scholarship Fund has offered scholarships and support services to single parents in NWA since 1984.[6] Because of its success, a statewide affiliate program was established in Arkansas. One of the products of this growth included the establishment of SPSF Benton County and SPSF Northwest Arkansas, serving Carroll, Madison, and Washington Counties. Both groups had the same mission, much of the same processes in place, with the only substantive difference being the geographic counties of clients being served. (If you're not familiar with NWA, Benton County is in NWA.) This geographic mash-up became problematic for scholarship applicants, donors, and the university systems in the region.

Fast-forward to 2021, when a decision was made that it was ultimately in everyone's best interests that the two organizations would become one. "We're better together" was the driving force.

But this change was no slam dunk. The merger had many details to contend with. What would the organization be called? How would they not confuse the donor base further? How would they not lose donors with a strong county affiliation? Who's on the board of directors? Who's in charge of marketing? Fundraising? Programs?

Time and space here don't allow for a full account of what

these leaders have done to create this exemplary success story, but here are some things they did to work through the merger of the two well-established, high-functioning organizations:

- The boards were merged, with a new board chair selected. Additionally, they went through a designed board formation exercise to accelerate their ability to function effectively to build relationships, understand who was bringing what expertise and capacity to the table, and get aligned.
- A commitment was made that 100 percent of the staff would be retained. There was plenty of work to do. Titles and scope of work might change, but a seat on the bus was assured. With the exception of one retirement, everyone on both staffs stayed.
- A marketing firm was retained to establish a completely new brand strategy that launched the "new" organization.
- A strategic planning process was put in motion. One of the strategies owned by the COO focused on integration—team building, culture, meeting cadence, and the like. Specifics included quarterly team social events, a "positivity board" on the refrigerator, monthly lunch and learns, team service projects, a software tool to provide individual and team personality profiles, team engagement surveys, and job tools.

This is just a snapshot of things they've done over the last two years. Was it seamless? Probably not. Have they done an outstanding job of it? Absolutely. I've had the privilege of being among the resources they were able to pull into this effort.

Still not convinced of their story's relevance to your truth? Consider these moving parts:

- Revenue
- Expenses
- Process and workflow
- Organizational design
- Culture
- Marketing and branding
- Governance
- Customer experience
- Strategy
- Team member engagement and retention
- Stakeholder interests

But this is the section about the leader's role, right? Tyler B. Clark, the president and CEO of the unified organization, was instrumental in building the bridges for all of these factors to work. He got the support from the board to know governance would be strong. He received support to pursue the outside help he would need. He built relationships with team members that he'd not previously known and took his existing relationships with team members to a new context, integrating a new set of peers he'd count on to do their work. He was able to get buy-in that "we will be and now are better together."

"We worked with seven subcommittees for over eighteen months to build the best organization possible," Clark said. "At the beginning of each meeting, we would reflect on why the merger was the right move. Whether we had a guest speaker or a 'mission moment,' the point was to have the outcome be the most significant impact on our recipients/clients. There is no doubt that two years later, all the hard work paid off, and we are a stronger organization, serving more people."

The Tone and Message in Acquisition

As we've established, tone and message are vital components in terms of what we want our team members to believe. In each case, they must be authentic. People can see through lip service. Trust, clarity, and unity don't come easily. Add repetition and deep personal commitment to authenticity, and you're on your way.

Let's look at an example from the past that we can learn from today. As the anticipation for the end of the Civil War began growing, President Abraham Lincoln faced many issues of reunification. This wasn't just an acquisition or even a reacquisition of what had been temporarily lost. War had been waged. Tens of thousands of lives were lost. Property had been destroyed. Families were divided. And, there was a winner and a loser. Papers had been signed, and not of a transactional purchase or buyout. This was surrender with terms issued. Further, throughout history, the rule of war was "to the victor belong the spoils." For many in the North, it was time to make the South pay the price for their insubordination. But President Lincoln was not among them.

Lincoln acted swiftly, purposefully, and repetitively for a conciliatory reunification for the United States of America. He even began to do so before General Lee's surrender at Appomattox on April 9, 1865.

- The closing line of the Gettysburg Address is "that this nation, under God, shall have a new birth of freedom—and that government of the people, by the people, for the people, shall not perish from the earth."[7]
- On December 8, 1863, Lincoln announced his Proclamation of Amnesty and Reconstruction that included a full pardon and restoration of property for those involved in the rebellion with the exception of the highest-ranking officers in the Confederacy; a plan for the reestablishment of state government; and an interim plan to address slavery.
- The Wade-Davis Bill was created as many legislators thought Lincoln's terms for reconstruction to be too

lenient, and although Congress passed the bill, Lincoln declined to sign it into law, effectively killing the bill with a pocket veto.[8]
- In his second inaugural address on March 4, 1865, Lincoln said, "With malice toward none with charity for all with firmness in the right as God gives us to see the right let us strive on to finish the work we are in to bind up the nation's wounds, to care for him who shall have borne the battle and for his widow and his orphan—to do all which may achieve and cherish a just and lasting peace among ourselves and with all nations." Historians further called out his intentional use of the words "we" and "us" over "I" and "me."[9]

Lincoln would be assassinated in April 1865, and while he never fully saw his reunification vision come to pass, and while more conservative Republicans found ways to impose stronger sanctions against the South, Lincoln's role in reunification (read: acquisition) is widely recognized through an unmistakable tone.

Clearly an argument can be made for tone. But doesn't the message vary by context? Probably. One could argue that if the message is too generic ("Can't we all just get along?"), it will fall short and potentially be impotent in providing the clarity necessary for buy-in. Thus, it follows that we should be looking for a construct on how to craft the message itself. Is there a template? Let me offer one.

In my time at Soderquist Leadership, our director of experiential learning relayed this construct, which is a fundamental structure to facilitate a debrief of a shared experience:

- What? (What just happened? What was our experience?)
- So what? (Why is that important? Or what's important about it? What part of this is relevant and matters?)

- Now what? (Given that, what do we do now? What are the forward implications? How do we take the insights and learning and apply them?)

Applying this construct to the season of Acquisition could provide that accelerant to clarity, trust, and buy-in. Let's take a look based on the anecdotes in this chapter:

1. We just bought Scott Paper.
2. This helps strengthen our tissue business in target markets and brings strong recognized brands into our portfolio.
3. We need to reconcile the K-C heritage and Scott heritage systems and ways of working to optimize our work.

AND

1. We are merging with another group that does the same thing we do, just in a different set of counties.
2. This helps reduce confusion, eliminates redundancy, and ultimately makes us more effective in our relationships with our scholarship recipients and our university partners.
3. We're launching a new organization with a new identity and a strong history. We need to reconcile our processes. We need to bring the public with us on why this makes sense.

Notice that the construct is not adequate to hold the exhaustive detail of everything that needs to happen, and that's OK. It more closely resembles an elevator pitch. Its effectiveness is rooted in reflection, simplicity, and its ability to bring people forward into their new reality.

Belief in Acquisition

Just as the principals in an acquisition believe "we're better together," so must the rest of both organizations. If the principals didn't believe it, they wouldn't have made the deal. For the deal to work, or at least achieve its maximum potential, all of the team members need to believe that. Otherwise, opportunity will get left on the table. As in my experience through the Scott Paper acquisition, I bought into the idea that it was a smart move, and any growing pains we could expect to (and did) experience were worth the effort. Granted, this was probably easier for me as part of the acquiring firm, especially given that my job was largely unaffected. Had I been a Scott team member, or if my job was among those changed—or even lost, I likely would have felt much differently.

Note, too, that this "we're better together" belief also extends outside the newly merged firm. You can bet Wall Street's belief mattered in the K-C/Scott deal. And as we've established, our competition, P&G and others, also adopted some beliefs about it. Continue that thread and you can bet our customers (i.e., retailers) needed to believe the new organization was better and in their interests. Also in line were our suppliers, some of whom were probably shared between K-C and Scott, and others that may have been introduced to new opportunities through the deal. Last, but certainly not least, were the consumers. Not for a moment do I think they cared about operational efficiencies, sales strategy, and the rest, but we did need them to maintain their beliefs about our brands as we introduced a massive brand migration strategy in our markets. The last thing we needed was to lose share to Puffs or Charmin because it was perceived that something had changed (for the worse).

Acquisitions, as seamless as we try to make them, at some level do introduce change—and with change, every stakeholder is evaluating WIIFM (what's in it for me?). If there's threat of loss, it must be addressed. If there's lack of clarity, it needs to be provided. If there's an upside, we can't have people miss it. Likely, there are trade-offs, and you're hoping in all of it that the net is for people to reach the principals' consensus: "We're better together."

FOR REFLECTION

1. Do your people have appropriate line of sight and context to be as excited about your mergers/acquisitions as you are as a leader?

2. What anxiety, resentment, and trust issues have spun up in the staff naturally because of the change forced upon them? How might you help people work through those things where it might have merit? How might you curb breakdown in areas that are unnecessary?

3. What stage in Tuckman's model are you currently in? Could it vary within the company? What are the causes that have brought you to this place? What will it take for you to get to the next stage, closer toward Performing?

In the message you need to send, what is your "What? So what? Now what?" Are you stating it clearly and consistently? Does your tone fit the message? Are you being consistent with it as well?

CHAPTER 9

COMPOUNDING

In the introduction, I asserted that a common seasonal theme of spring-summer-fall-winter is inadequate to address the dynamics at play in the seasons of a given organization's life cycle. Having now offered an alternative model, breaking down familiar seasons that I, and likely you, have experienced, I must confess the handling of the model is incomplete so far. Here's why.

In the preceding eight chapters, each season has been treated independent of any other season and the factors it could bring. My experience suggests that this is in fact a pretty common experience. Yet, I also know that it is entirely possible, and even likely, that you will experience compounding seasons, where different seasons layer on top of each other.

If it were food, we'd call it fusion. If it were music, we'd call it a mash-up. These compounding factors create a compounding level of complexity that demands a compounded approach. Still, the working hypothesis is that the model holds. Let's test it.

Going back to the structure, a season will have:

1. Factors at play that characterize the reality of what's being experienced. These are descriptive and have dimension.

2. These factors call for focus and activity appropriate to the context.
3. The leader will assume a role, also appropriate to this context.
4. The leader adopts a message and tone . . .
5. In order to get people to believe something so that they will buy in to what needs to be done.

Compounding seasons don't affect the logic structure. They just add new layers, with each one demanding that all five components be addressed.

Here's a simple, two-layered example from my early career. In 1999, Pampers launched a line extension called Pampers Rash Guard that made an over-the-counter (OTC) drug claim that it could treat and prevent diaper rash. This was a super-premium diaper that quickly gained a meaningful share of a highly competitive disposable diaper market and took a direct shot at Kimberly-Clark's Huggies Supreme diaper. It was a clear case of External Disruption.

At the time, I was a young operations team leader working in a feminine care facility for K-C, making Class I and Class II medical devices, a business highly regulated by the FDA. I had also led our quality team and was by then intimately aware of the FDA's Code of Federal Regulations and how we complied with them in our operations.

In order to respond to the competitive threat, we fully intended to launch our own diaper with a feature that would allow us to make the same OTC claim to compete with the new Pampers diaper. While I was never told this, I imagined a conversation that went something like this:

"We need to find someone who knows how we operate our plants and more about the FDA."
"Well, there's this kid in Arkansas . . ."

This was equivalent to a minor leaguer playing Class A ball getting his call to "The Show" in the middle of a pennant race. Here, we introduce a second compounding season of Readiness.

I will never forget my first team meeting, my first week after my move to headquarters. In the room was Tom, our VP; Terry, our director; and my "peers," Mike, Susan, Simon, Carlos, Dave, and Kevin. I put peers in quotes because while we all occupied the same tier on the org chart, I was anything but a peer to the talent and experience in the room. I remember thinking, *Holy crap, I'm the weak link.*

I also remember saying something incredibly stupid in that meeting and immediately thinking to myself, *What an idiot!*

What we were going to try to do was the regulatory equivalent to Maverick running the course in 2:15. Yet, I remember the confidence being placed in me throughout that project. Still in my twenties, I was consulting and directing leaders far more experienced than I was in what we needed to do to be successful.

As a leader, you undoubtedly can think of examples of your own compounding seasons. You probably don't have to think much past the COVID-19 pandemic. Talk about External Disruption, Crisis, Trough, and potentially Readiness, plus any other seasons not addressed in this book. Layer upon layer. Factor on factor. Focus upon focus. Message upon message. An unprecedented tone and a belief that we never thought we'd have to conjure.

So, when we think about the model applied to compounding seasons, as we've indicated, the five components hold. The added complexity sparked by the compounding seasons would demand a more sophisticated assessment of the situation and a more sophisticated, multifaceted, concurrent response of leadership. It might require drawing on the experience of more people. It might require more time, patience, monitoring, and adjustments. Predictably, it would require more effort in communication as things change and we make sense of it. In all, the model can still be a tool to structure our thinking and our actions in any combination or context.

FOR REFLECTION

1. Looking back on your career, when have you experienced a compounding of seasons? How did this affect your response in leadership compared to any one season being active on its own?

2. What relevant business factors do you anticipate would take priority in a given compounded scenario? How do these align with your organizational and/or personal values?

3. How have you been able to apply lessons learned from prior seasons to new seasons?

A FINAL THOUGHT

From the outset, my presentation of this model was a hypothesis to test. By now, you probably have judged its validity at some level, and I'm OK with that. Again, that is kind of the point. The bigger point in my personal goal of constructive provocation is anything you and your organization would glean and, most importantly, apply.

For this model and the supporting stories to have any value, and for you to redeem your investment in reading this book, it's up to you to employ it in real time and space, with real stakes on the table.

It's my hope that in doing so, you will sharpen your organization, the leaders in your care, and your own leadership muscle—and that you will, in turn, be able to pass your experiences on to others for their gain.

Godspeed.

ENDNOTES

Introduction: Situations or Seasons?
1. Wikipedia, s.v. "Situational Leadership Theory," last modified May 2, 2023, https://en.wikipedia.org/wiki/Situational_leadership_theory.
2. Ecclesiastes 1:9.
3. Proverbs 27:17.

Chapter 1: The Model
1. The Byrds, "Turn! Turn! Turn!" 1965.
2. Andrew Steadman, "Seasons in Leadership," The Military Leader, https://themilitaryleader.com/seasons-leadership/.
3. Wikipedia, s.v. "OODA loop," last modified July 1, 2023, https://en.wikipedia.org/wiki/OODA_loop.

Chapter 2: External Disruption
1. Wikipedia, s.v. *"Who Moved My Cheese?,"* last modified June 8, 2023, https://en.wikipedia.org/wiki/Who_Moved_My_Cheese%3F.
2. Lauren Thomas, "Here's the One Photo Walmart's CEO Keeps on His Phone to Stoke 'Healthy Paranoia' in Race Against Amazon," *CNBC.com*, December 7, 2018, https://www.cnbc.com/2018/12/07/walmarts-ceo-says-this-photo-inspires-him-to-stay-ahead-of-amazon.html.
3. Eddy Malik, "Amazon History Timeline," July 3, 2017, https://www.officetimeline.com/blog/amazon-history-timeline.
4. Tricia McKinnon, "6 Reasons Walmart's eCommerce Strategy Is Winning," Indigo Digital, March 9, 2023, https://www.indigo9digital.com/blog/4-secrets-to-walmarts-ecommerce-sucess.
5. Alfonso Segura, "Strategic Acquisitions: Amazon vs Walmart," The Fashion Retailer, November 13, 2017, https://fashionretail.blog/2017/11/13/4485/.
6. Nick Statt, "Amazon and Walmart's Rivalry Is Reshaping How We'll Buy Everything in the Future," The Verge, August 3, 2018, https://www.theverge.com/2018/8/3/17630604/amazon-walmart-competition-tech-partnerships-grocery-delivery.

7. Mark Kolakowski, "Why Amazon's Biggest Threat May Be Wal-Mart," *Investopedia*, May 2, 2021, https://www.investopedia.com/news/why-amazons-biggest-threat-may-be-walmart/.
8. Lauren Thomas, "Amazon Isn't Killing Walmart Online," *CNBC.com*, February 19, 2019, https://www.cnbc.com/2019/02/19/amazon-isnt-killing-walmart-online.html.
9. "Walmart's Strategy to Beat Amazon Prime," eTail Palm Springs 2024 Blog, https://etailwest.wbresearch.com/blog/walmarts-strategy-to-beat-amazon-prime.
10. McMillon.

Chapter 3: Internal Disruption
1. Jim Collins, *Good to Great* (New York: HarperCollins, 2001).
2. Charles Handy, *The Empty Raincoat: Making Sense of the Future* (London: Arrow Books, 1995), 50–57.
3. John P. Kotter, *Leading Change* (Brighton, MA: Harvard Business Review Press, 2012).
4. Wikipedia, s.v. "We choose to go to the Moon," last modified July 21, 2023, https://en.wikipedia.org/wiki/We_choose_to_go_to_the_Moon.
5. Hugo Young, Bryan Silcock, Peter M. Dunn, *Journey to Tranquility* (London: Jonathon Cape, 1969), 109–112.
6. Jeanie Daniel Duck, *The Change Monster: The Human Forces That Fuel or Foil Corporate Transformation and Change* (New York: Three Rivers Press, 2002), 16–17.

Chapter 4: Crisis
1. Wikipedia, s.v. "The Blitz," last modified July 9, 2023, https://en.wikipedia.org/wiki/The_Blitz.
2. Jon Meacham, *Franklin and Winston* (New York: Random House, 2003), 36.
3. Greg Bustin, *How Leaders Decide* (Naperville, IL: Sourcebooks, 2019), 78.
4. Bustin, 79.
5. Winston Churchill, "We Shall Fight on the Beaches," International Churchill Society, June 4, 1940, https://winstonchurchill.org/resources/speeches/1940-the-finest-hour/we-shall-fight-on-the-beaches/.

6. Winston Churchill, "Never Give In, Never, Never, Never, 1941," National Churchill Museum, October 29, 1941, https://www.nationalchurchillmuseum.org/never-give-in-never-never-never.html.
7. Meacham, 51–52.
8. Bill George, *Seven Lessons for Leading in Crisis* (San Francisco: Jossey-Bass, 2009).
9. Hebrews 11:1.

Chapter 5: Readiness
1. Joseph Kosinski, director, *Top Gun: Maverick* (Hollywood, CA: Paramount Pictures, 2022).
2. Carol Dweck, "The Power of Believing You Can Improve," TED, https://www.ted.com/talks/carol_dweck_the_power_of_believing_that_you_can_improve.
3. Theodore Melfi, director, *Hidden Figures* (Los Angeles: Fox 2000 Pictures, 2016).
4. Margot Lee Shetterly, "Dorothy Vaughan Biography," NASA.gov, https://www.nasa.gov/content/dorothy-vaughan-biography/.
5. Wikipedia, s.v. "Dorothy Vaughan," last modified July 24, 2003, https://en.wikipedia.org/wiki/Dorothy_Vaughan.
6. Wikipedia, s.v. "Dorothy Vaughan."
7. "Modern Figures: Frequently Asked Questions," NASA.gov, https://www.nasa.gov/modernfigures/faq.

Chapter 6: Peak
1. Wikipedia, s.v. *Joseph and the Amazing Technicolor Dreamcoat*, last modified August 13, 2023, https://en.wikipedia.org/wiki/Joseph_and_the_Amazing_Technicolor_Dreamcoat.
2. Dr. Spencer Johnson, *Who Moved My Cheese?* (London: Vermilion, 1999).
3. Kevin P. Kearns, "From Comparative Advantage to Damage Control: Clarifying Strategic Issues Using SWOT Analysis," *Nonprofit Management and Leadership* 3, no. 1 (Fall 1992): 3–22.
4. Genesis 41:49.
5. Genesis 41:57.
6. Chick-fil-A 2009 case study used with permission.

7. Matt Kempner, "Chick-fil-A Passes CEO Title to Third Generation of Cathy Family," *The Atlanta Journal-Constitution*, September 16, 2021, https://www.ajc.com/news/business/chick-fil-a-passes-ceo-title-to-third-generation-of-cathy-family/HLRODFCSPRFTPAHDSJAD5CGVDY/.

Chapter 7: Trough

1. "Circular Flow Diagram," Lumen, https://courses.lumenlearning.com/suny-oldwestbury-publicfinanceandpublicpolicy/chapter/circular-flow-diagram/.
2. "Little Village," Choose Chicago, https://www.choosechicago.com/neighborhoods/little-village/.
3. Wikipedia, s.v. "Serenity Prayer," last modified May 28, 2023, https://en.wikipedia.org/wiki/Serenity_Prayer.
4. "Problem Solving and Decision Making," Kepner-Tregoe, https://kepner-tregoe.com/training/problem-solving-decision-making/.
5. "Vice Admiral James Bond Stockdale—USNA, Annapolis, Md.," Waymark, https://www.waymarking.com/waymarks/wm526T_Vice_Admiral_James_Bond_Stockdale_USNA_Annapolis_Md.
6. "The Stockdale Paradox," Jim Collins, https://www.jimcollins.com/concepts/Stockdale-Concept.html.
7. Alfred Lansing, *Endurance* (New York: Basic Books, 2014).
8. Martin Luther King Jr., "Remaining Awake Through a Great Revolution," Smithsonian Institution, March 31, 1968, https://www.si.edu/spotlight/mlk?page=4&iframe=true#:~:text=We%20shall%20overcome%20because%20the,Cathedral%2C%20March%2031%2C%201968.

Chapter 8: Acquisition

1. Glenn Collins, "Kimberly-Clark to Buy Scott Paper, Challenging P.&G.," *New York Times*, July 18, 1995, https://www.nytimes.com/1995/07/18/business/kimberly-clark-to-buy-scott-paper-challenging-p-g.html.
2. Wikipedia, s.v. "Albert J. Dunlap," last modified June 26, 2023, https://en.wikipedia.org/wiki/Albert_J._Dunlap.
3. Blooomberg Business News, "P.&G. to Acquire a Baby Products Unit of Scott," *New York Times*, May 24, 1996, https://www.nytimes.com/1996/05/24/business/p-g-to-acquire-a-baby-products-unit-of-scott.html.

4. Emma-Louise, Tuckman's 5 Stages of Team Development Model and How to Use It," The Coaching Tools Company.com, https://www.thecoachingtoolscompany.com/get-your-team-performing-beautifully-with-this-powerful-group-development-model/.
5. Peter Segal, director, *Tommy Boy* (Hollywood, CA: Paramount Pictures, 1995).
6. "History," Single Parent Scholarship Fund of Northwest Arkansas, https://spsfnwa.org/history/.
7. "Gettysburg Address," National Geographic Education, https://education.nationalgeographic.org/resource/gettysburg-address/.
8. "Wade-Davis Bill (1864)," National Archives, https://www.archives.gov/milestone-documents/wade-davis-bill.
9. "'With Malice Toward None . . .': Lincoln's Second Inaugural Address," National Park Service, https://www.nps.gov/articles/000/-with-malice-toward-none-lincoln-s-second-inaugural.htm.

ACKNOWLEDGEMENTS

For years, the idea of writing a book was something that sounded like it could be fun and even an important thing to do, but nothing I ever really considered seriously or for which I had a plan. It was just something that was rolling around in my mind. And yet, here we are. This experience has been one of both high effort and high learning.

I am fortunate to have access to accomplished writers like Dr. Steve Graves, Stephen Caldwell, Mark Zweig, and Greg Bustin, each of whom has done this work and was extraordinarily generous in their sharing their experience and encouraged me to take the leap.

Thanks to Karen Pickering and the team at Book Villages. Without her encouragement and the expertise of a been-there-done-that publisher, I simply could not have completed this project.

I've been blessed beyond measure to have had access to accomplished leaders, from those on a global stage to those at the local point-of-contact. The ability to draw on their experiences have animated the model I've tried to put forward. Thank you to Tim and the team at Chick-fil-A, Harold, and Tyler for permission to relay your stories alongside the others drawn from the public domain that give this book its life.

To the team we had at Soderquist Leadership—it was a remarkable collection of character, drive, and experience that gave life to a terrific season of work and learning. So much of what's shared in this book was influenced by that time and each of you. I'll always be indebted to the investment you made and the grace you offered in our time together. Thanks to Tom Melson who gave me my shot at the big leagues at Kimberly-Clark and to John Costello who was so much more than a boss in an incredibly formative time in my career.

A special thanks to Lucas, Judy, Aaron, Lori, Donny, Steve, and Kai for their review and input on the chapters as I wrote. Your investment made the final work sharper, clearer, and smarter. I value your experience but more so your friendship. Thanks to Stacey, Charles, and David for coming along later in the process with those above and were willing to put your stamp on the work in the form of an endorsement.

I am thankful to my Lord and Savior, Jesus Christ. I recognize that "every good and perfect gift comes from above" (James 1:17) and this book is an attempt at stewarding the gifts I've been given through my professional career.

Finally, to my high school sweetheart who agreed to be my bride all those years ago, you simultaneously anchor and encourage me, beyond what I deserve or can even comprehend. I love you.

ABOUT THE AUTHOR

Chuck Hyde is a trusted advisor to CEOs, key executives and emerging leaders. He has a track record of building teams, acquiring and maximizing talent, developing strategy and delivering results. He is the Founder and Principal of C3 Advisors, LLC., a private consulting practice launched in 2017 focused on executive leadership and talent optimization.

Chuck's professional career started in the Fortune 100 with Kimberly-Clark Corporation. An operator at heart, he spent eight years in manufacturing plants and four years in staff roles supporting them. His roles included engineering, regulatory compliance, quality systems, operations, and project management. Chuck spent the next twelve years in the consulting industry with Soderquist Leadership—his last eight as CEO. Chuck then served for four years as a Chair for private peer advisory boards through Vistage Worldwide.

When he's not with his family or clients, you can find him on his road bike or the golf course.

To learn more about Chuck, his work, or to contact him, visit www.c3adv.com.